Lexington, Bedfo... ...cord

Ghosts, Legends, and Lore

E. Ashley Rooney

Schiffer Publishing Ltd

4880 Lower Valley Road, Atglen, Pennsylvania 19310

Cover photo: On the hillside overlooking Concord's Monument Square is the original burying ground for Concord residents, known as the Old Hill Burying Ground. The earliest existing stone is dated 1677. *Courtesy of Siobhan Theriault*

Floral©Thomas Villarreal. Image from BigStockPhoto.com.

Copyright © 2009
by E. Ashley Rooney
Library of Congress
Control Number:
2008934030

Designed by Stephanie Daugherty
Type set in Rosemary Roman/ NewBskvll BT

ISBN: 978-0-7643-3115-2
Printed in China

Photograph: Lexington Minuteman. Courtesy of Peter Lund

Dedication

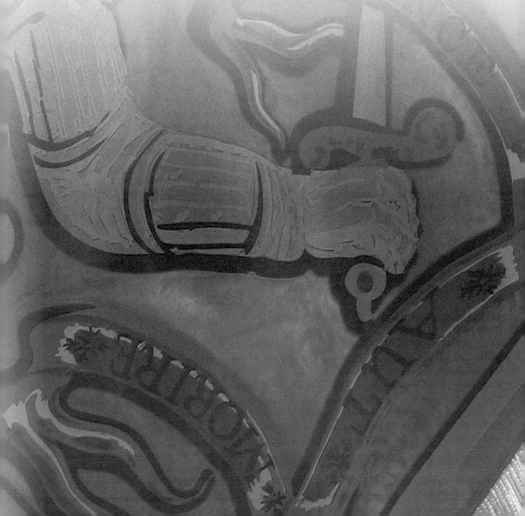

exington, Massachusetts, is where Revere and his cohorts shouted, "The regulars are coming." It was where Sam Adams said, "What a glorious morning for America." It was where the first blood of the American Revolution was shed. Concord is renowned as the site of the battle of North Bridge, where the Americans first tasted victory. Between these two towns lies Bedford, home of the first American flag carried into battle, and the Battle Road. This book is dedicated to our forefathers and to the freedoms that we enjoy today.

Acknowledgements

I was delighted when S. Levi Doran decided to research Lexington ghosts. It's obvious that one day he will be a history professor. Betsy Johnston, my wonderful cousin, and Barbara Purchia, a new friend, encouraged, edited, and proofed the manuscript. Then there's Dinah Roseberry of Schiffer, who makes me feel like I know what I'm doing. Finally, the photography of Peter Lund, Paul Doherty, and Siobhan Theriault certainly helps illustrate my stories.

Contents

Part One:
Ghosts

*H*ave *you*
ever had the hair
at the nape of your neck
prickle uneasily when you heard
the creak of a stair or felt a sudden
chill in the room? All areas have ghosts.
The Lexington and Concord areas not only
have ghosts, but these locales have ghosts of many
patriotic men and women. Statues and monuments
to their heroism can be found throughout the area. The
ghostly tales that follow endeavor to give these spirits a
past, a present, and perhaps even a future.

A Glorious Day for America

E ven when I was a little girl, I had a crush on Jonathan Harrington. I found him strong, brave, and quite dashing. Ultimately, he asked me—me, little Ruth Fisk—to marry him, and when our son, Johnny, was born in 1766, I thought my heart would burst with joy.

We were married for six years when Jonathan came home with a big grin on his face. He kissed me heartily, clasping his large hands around my waist. "I have a surprise for you."

"Kiss me first, then tell me." He took me in his arms, pulling me close and kissed me hard. Then he pulled me down next to him.

"What do you think of this red, by the way?" I pointed at the yarn in my spinning wheel. "I found some pokeberries and thought I could make you and your handsome son matching red shirts."

"It's beautiful, my dear, but guess what? Thomas Perry is nervous about the events in Boston and wants to leave Lexington. According to him, there is going to be trouble." Certainly, the British and the Patriots seemed to be having a battle of wills. About eighteen months ago, armed British soldiers had fired on a crowd of Bostonians, killing five unarmed men. Mobs of citizens had been taunting and teasing the British soldiers—even throwing snowballs—for several months until a British officer ordered the shooting when he thought the rabble rousers were out of control. Five unarmed patriots were killed; the soldiers were arrested and charged. John Adams defended them, and all but two were found innocent. To us, that meant that American justice could be as fair-minded as British justice. "What kind of trouble?" I asked doubtfully.

"Thomas has heard that war might break out between us and the British, and he wants to move back to Royalston and sell his house here in the village. You know, the house...It's the one that the widow Abigail owned before him—the woman who kept the poor house for the town. I think we should buy it."

"The one on the Common? Oh, Jonathan, we would be close to the meetinghouse and the school. Please let's buy it. *This was exciting,* I thought. I was tired of living so far away from my neighbors. The only time I got to see anyone was at Sunday meeting. Now I could see more of my friends. They could come for tea. And young Johnny would have some friends.

"Yes, that one. We would be right in the center. The house is good and has a large plot of good land."

"And you don't think there's going to be a war, do you? Everything is going to be all right?"

"Of course, my dear. We are together, and I'm here to protect you and Johnny."

So Jonathan, Johnny, and I bought the house facing the Common. It had a large plot behind it where Jonathan planned to grow corn, squash, turnips, parsnips, carrots, and pumpkins. I wanted to have a small herb garden readily accessible to the kitchen door for my chamomile, garlic, and hyssop.

For quite a few years, the house had withstood the winter nor'easters and the rain-pounding winds. The fireplace was so high that I could stand in it. It would be the heart and soul of my family. I could suckle my babes here—more babies—please God let there be at least one girl child. My beautiful hand-hewn cradle would be filled again. I would make my bread there, heat our soup, and we would keep ourselves warm when the earth stood hard as iron and snow fell upon snow.

I would place my big four-poster with its canopy against the front wall so we could look out on the meadow. The big blanket chest would go under the window and a clothes cupboard beside it. From here would come the warmth, the companionship, and the love that we would need to survive.

Jonathan moved his mare, a yoke of oxen, six steers, four cows, three fat pigs, some assorted chickens, his plow, and a cart. I packed our clothes and two black sheep skins, our kitchen earthenware, my English pewter and brassware, wooden vessels, and house linens. We transported our belongings in a two-wheeled ox cart. Hay and straw supplied the packing, but the roads were rough and rocky, and I worried whether all would be transported safely. Finally, we arrived with the great chests of drawers, the high-backed chairs, the linen chests, and the various tables.

And so we moved to our new home. Jonathan applied new cedar shakes to the old roof, replaced the broken bricks in the kitchen fireplace, and found fresh timber for the decaying sills. I scrubbed the floors with sand, cleaned out the mouse nests, and scraped the fireplace clean of old ashes, saving them to make soap the next time. Four-year-old Johnny brought in the kindling, fed the pigs, and collected the eggs. The neighbors came to visit. It was wonderful.

Jonathan and I worked hard. As soon as one set of chores was done, another set came along. Life was busy with its necessities. We grew many vegetables, strawberries, and raspberries. We planted apple trees. Jonathan shot the occasional deer and wild turkeys. The cows needed milking, the eggs needed collecting, the vegetables needed picking. When the animals no longer produced milk or eggs, Jonathan slaughtered them, and we salted, smoked, or pickled the meat so it wouldn't spoil. We used the hide for leather breeches, the bones for buttons, and the fat for soap. *Waste not, want not*, I said to myself, as I stood over the boiling pot of fat that would eventually become soap.

Now that we were in the center of town, I joined in the quilting, sewing, and all the other types of bees that brought the womenfolk together and served to lighten the drudgery of our work. We talked and laughed as we worked, piecing out new quilts, hemming our garments, and darning the socks.

We planted a flower garden with foxgloves, sweet William, yellow and orange lilies, and, of course, my all-essential herb garden. The years passed, and life was good, except there were no more babies. I had just the one: my precious Johnny named after his dashing father. And he was that. Each night I would read from the Bible or *Pilgrim's Progress* to Johnny; then he would go to bed, and Jonathan and I would have our own

The privately owned Harrington House facing the Lexington Green still stands today.
Courtesy of Paul E. Doherty

time. He still made me feel on fire with the way he brushed my hair back from my face and touched my skin with such sureness. He would put his arms around me, and I could hardly breathe for I loved him so much.

No matter how hard he worked, Jonathan was always there for me. I could feel my heart melting as I watched his large hands brush back his hair and his blue eyes twinkle at me. Sometimes, I would have this urge to touch his sunburned neck and kiss that soft spot in his throat where a pulse beat. I wanted to hold him and take comfort in his warmth. I snuggled in his arms and lay on his brawny chest and felt his tender hands in my hair. We may not have had any more babies, but we had the three of us and that was good enough for me.

Johnny followed his father like a puppy, practically treading on his heels. He almost wagged in delight when Jonathan let him carry a bucket of water from the well or bring in fuel for the day or feed the swine. Once, despite all my cleaning, he found a mouse nest behind the fireplace. He brought it to me:

a mound of sheep's wool and shreds of sacking, woven together. Three tiny dun-colored mice with long pink tails squirmed. I smiled. "Let's put it out in the barn but be sure to keep the cats away." Johnny was devoted to his mice. He would have been a good big brother, but I was beginning to accept that all we would have was Johnny.

Like most New England villages, Lexington clustered about a green, which was the heart of the center—and its conscience. The meetinghouse was at one end, and Reverend Clarke's sermons were the event of the week. Afterwards, we would go to the tavern to discuss the sermon and measure our thoughts against those of others.

As the snow appeared like a ghost in the silent night and shrouded the fields and hills in a soft white blanket that December, the Lexington citizens expressed their anger about the British rule and the repressive taxes of sugar, stamps, and other necessities imposed by the English Parliament. Reverend Clarke, who had family connections to John Hancock, knew a good deal about what was happening in Boston. He told us about the speeches that men were making in Boston and the tension that was rising between the "provincials" or "Yankees" and the British regulars.

A visitor to town that December told us about the Boston Tea Party. We laughed as he described how the Sons of Liberty colored their faces copper with paint, donned feathered headdresses, and covered themselves with buckskin and blankets. He said they went down to the wharf while the crowd listened to Samuel Adams. Once the meeting ended, the crowd joined them at the wharf, where so-called Indians boarded the East India merchantmen, smashed open the tea chests, and dumped the tea overboard. The tea even stained the water a deep brown, he said.

So although I had the neighbors in, there was no more tea—unless we made 'Labrador tea' from a small, aromatic shrub with narrow, leathery leaves. I put it in my pewter pot, and we all pretended that it was good.

Buckman Tavern at 1 Bedford Street, Lexington, was a favorite rendezvous for townsfolk. After sitting for most of Sunday in an unheated meetinghouse, residents came here for hot flip, a warm fire, and social interaction. In the early hours of April 19, members of the Lexington militia waited here for the British regulars. The Lexington Historical Society has restored Buckman Tavern, which it bought in 1913. A costumed guide tells stories about that time and show guests the kitchen, ladies' parlor, and landlord's bedroom. Many historic items are on display. *Courtesy of Paul E. Doherty*

Life went on. Jonathan was becoming more proficient at blacksmithing and made some lovely twisted candlesticks. We had more cows and more pigs. Johnny had learned how to milk the cows. The apple trees we had planted were beginning to produce, and young Johnny, growing tall and straight like a young sapling, was learning well at school.

On Sundays after meeting, discussions at the tavern would get quite heated. Many colonists thought we must meet force with force. The town's militia practiced more; of course, Jonathan was a part of that.

Then in late fall of 1774, as the first sleet was sifting through the forest branches and rattling through the frozen leaves, the provincial Congress of Massachusetts created a Committee of Safety, collected gunpowder and weapons, and revived the old New England training bands. All men between the ages of sixteen and fifty were asked to enlist themselves in the militia.

Older men were organized into a group called the alarm list. The Provincial Congress also recommended that one quarter of the militia be organized in minute companies ready to march at the shortest notice.

Meanwhile, the force of Redcoats in Boston had increased considerably. "I tell you, Ruth," said Jonathan over supper one night, "watching this is like watching a fire. It started with only a few small sparks, but now it is burning faster and higher—so much so that it just can't go out on its own."

I put down my darning, held out my arms to Jonathan, and said, "If that's so, let's go to bed now, dear, and appreciate what we do have on this cold March night." He smiled, smoothed back my hair, and stood up, grasping my hand. "What a wonderful idea."

At meeting, Reverend Clarke told us to be ready too. "We need to sacrifice our estates and everything dear in life, yea and life itself, in support of the common cause." I certainly didn't want to sacrifice everything dear in my life—I wasn't even sure that I could sacrifice a cow for the common cause. "It's wrong," Reverend Clarke said, "to submit to a government which curtails citizens' rights and uses its power to reduce the colonists to the status of enslaved economic subjects without their normal rights of citizenship."

After meeting, people went to the tavern and sat at the long plank tables, drinking their flip, and talking about what this all meant. The talk was all about the possibility of war and when the colonies would declare themselves for independence. My neighbor kept muttering that the gun was cocked. "This will be a historic conflict that will divide English-speaking people one from another," said he, shaking his head sorrowfully.

I didn't see how we could fight the British. We were a peaceful town. We were just ordinary folks, and there's no way that we could stop an army. Besides, the British were the same as us. We had the same blood; we spoke the same language. We'd been tied to them for more than 150 years.

The frosty wind moaned, and the month of March dragged past. Bostonians were moving out of Boston and into outlying areas. Samuel Adams and John Hancock, the wealthiest man in the area, often visited with the Reverend Clarke down on Hancock Street.

I asked Jonathan if we should leave town, but he replied that we had to stay and stand and fight for freedom. "I can't let Johnny grow up this way—never able to control his life. We must fight for that right. You know that, Ruth. These are the reasons that our forebears came here."

I may have known it, but I certainly didn't want it to happen. I wanted to keep life from changing. Life was too precious to let it go.

April came with its mists and soft green blurs. One night, I was awakened by the sound of horse hooves. Lights began to flicker. I looked out and heard the rider shouting, "The regulars are coming out."

Jonathan came up behind me, pulling on his breeches over his nightshirt. "What are you doing at the window?"

I told him that I had heard a rider coming fast up Menotomy Road.

"I'm going to check on what's happening," Jonathan said, grabbing his musket, powder horn, and a lantern.

"Be careful." My heart beat madly.

"I'll come back and tell you what's going on," he promised.

When he returned, we sat around, those next hours worrying. He told me that earlier that day, the military governor of Massachusetts, General Thomas Gage, issued orders sending British troops under the command of Lieutenant Colonel Francis Smith and Marine Major John Pitcairn to Concord to destroy the military stores and supplies collected there. The plan was that 700 British regulars would leave Boston, cross the Charles River that night, and capture Samuel Adams and John Hancock, prominent leaders in the colonial cause who were visiting in Lexington. Following their capture, the troops were then to march to Concord and destroy the military supplies stored there. A relief column under the command of Lord Hugh Percy would leave six hours after the main column.

The Sons of Liberty in Boston had arranged for a signal. Should the British regulars move out by land over Boston Neck, one lantern was to be hung from the steeple of the North Church. If by sea, across the river, two lanterns were to be hung. The British selected the sea route, and Paul Revere set off for Lexington, a ride of nearly thirteen miles, to warn Hancock and Adams about the British movement. Having left Boston by the land route, William Dawes joined him, and they and other couriers roused the town leaders and militia commanders throughout the area that night.

When Revere reached Lexington and Reverend Clarke's house, he found eight men on guard under the command of Sergeant William Munroe.

"Don't make so much noise!" shouted Munroe as Revere galloped up to the gate.

"Noise!" repeated Revere. "You'll have noise enough here before long—the regulars are coming out." While he was talking to Hancock and Adams, William Dawes clattered up. With

Postcard courtesy of S. L. Doran; S. Lawrence Whipple, collector

The belfry bell sounded the alarm in Lexington on April 19, 1775. In 1775, the belfry was on the common behind the large meetinghouse. To this day, the Lexington belfry, located at the intersection of Massachusetts Avenue and Clarke Street, rings out the alarm in the early dawn of Patriots Day. *Courtesy of D. Peter Lund*

Revere in the lead, other messengers were dispatched from Lexington to the surrounding communities.

After Jonathan told me all this, he kissed me soundly. "I have to go out with the others." I could hear the belfry bell tolling over Lexington, calling the militia.

Militiamen were racing for the Common with their shirttails flapping. Captain Parker ordered them into ranks and instructed that their guns be charged with powder and ball. They waited for an hour, shivering in the night cold, until Captain Parker dismissed them, saying, "Come back at the beating of the drum." About half of the men went to Buckman Tavern for what they called "refreshments," but Jonathan came home to me. We tried to be casual with each other as if the muster was just one of those things that happened on an April night, but we didn't get any sleep that night. All night, bells rang, dogs barked, candles were lit, and muskets were loaded as we prepared for the next day.

Just before dawn on April 19, Captain Parker had teenage drummer William Diamond beat the call to arms. The town's belfry rang out the alarm. Ragged webs of morning fog blew across the Common. The street was muddy; the houses closed against the April chill. As the some seventy militia men, including my Jonathan, lined up in two long files, the distant sound of marching feet and shouted commands signaled the Redcoats' approach. The birds began to sing around the Common as they always do before dawn comes, but underlying their melodies was the sound of drums. Johnny and I could hear them tromp, tromp, tromping. It sounded like my heart. Soon the British column emerged through the morning fog. They were precision, glitter, and polish—the most formidable fighting force of the era. Our men looked ragtag compared to them.

Their scarlet coats shining, their bayonets gleaming, the British regulars marched up the road with practiced precision. First came the officers on horseback—then the color bearers, the drummers, and finally row after row of red uniforms stretching back down the road—back to the rising sun. In the dank early dawn, they marched onto the Common. Our men fell back. Johnny and I stood behind a tree near our front door. I could see my Jonathan standing boldly on the Common with the others. Jonas Parker stood with his hat on the ground filled with cartridges. My neighbors huddled in their doorways.

Captain Parker said, "Stand your ground. Don't fire unless fired upon, but if they mean to have a war let it begin here!"

Spurring his horse onto the Green, Major Pitcairn shouted, "Disperse. Lay down your arms, you damned rebels, and disperse." The soldiers marched past the drummers, wheeling and parading, while the officers reined in their prancing horses. Their faces looked small and cold. They looked so young under those white wigs.

Young Jonathan and I ran for our doorway. There was a silence, and then Captain Parker commanded his men to back off toward the Bedford Road. Many of them dispersed. Then I heard a single shot.

The regulars fired several volleys in return and charged— bayonets fixed. One part of me was screaming; the other was

The Battle of Lexington, Mass. The 19 of April 1775, Captain Parker drew up his company of seventy men on Lexington Green to await the approach of the British.

Postcard courtesy of S. L. Doran; S. Lawrence Whipple, collector

The fallen patriots. *Courtesy of Paul E. Doherty*

swooning. My whole world was ending in front of my eyes. When it was over, seven Americans lay dead: Jonas Parker was shot down at the second volley. As he lay there on the ground, a British soldier bayoneted him. Robert Munroe, the father of John and Ebenezer Munroe, was shot; he would have been sixty-three in several years. The others died as they attempted to respond to Pitcairn's order: young Isaac Muzzy was killed instantly; Samuel Hadley; John Brown; Ashabel Porter, and Caleb Harrington all died in that volley from the regulars. Most of the families in Lexington lost a relative or a friend in those brief moments on that April morning.

Opposite: Said to be the nation's oldest war memorial, Lexington's Revolutionary War Monument was installed on July 4, 1799, on the Lexington Common. In 1835, the remains of the eight men who were killed on April 19 were transferred from their common grave in Lexington's Old Burying Ground and placed in a tomb at the rear of the monument. The Revolutionary War monument on the Lexington Green has been at the forefront of historic events. It was here that French General Lafayette was welcomed to Lexington in 1824. It was here that World War I solders were bid farewell in 1917 and welcomed home in 1919. It was here that Lexington residents pledged to fight for liberty in World War II in 1942. Ceremonies are held here each Patriots Day. *Courtesy of D. Peter Lund*

But worse of all was my Jonathan. Wounded by British bullets, my dashing, loving Jonathan dragged himself to our doorway, where he died in my arms. He was only thirty-two. I collapsed in tears. Life as I knew it was gone. My wonderful Jonathan was no more.

The British suffered little. They fired a salute, gave three loud huzzahs, and resumed their march to Concord.

A year later, my son Johnny died at age ten. *Life is hard,* I tell myself. In 1777, I married John Smith of Boston, selling my wonderful home to my half brother Dr. David Fisk. He lived there as a newly wed and became a very busy man on the intersection. I didn't return during my lifetime. My life in Lexington was over.

Each year, since 1971, Jonathan and Ruth Fisk Harrington reappear on the Lexington Green as the events of April 19, 1775, are reenacted. Each year the dashing British come marching on to Lexington Common, where they are met by a small group of citizens who stand ready to defend their homes and their way of life. And each year Jonathan dies in Ruth's arms.

Recycling

When we were growing up, we played a lot of flashlight tag—up and down Meriam Hill and around the Common, although it had little cover. There was something so awesome about sneaking around, hiding, and then scaring or getting scared out of your mind. Of course, my mother wasn't happy when one neighbor complained that we had tromped through her Oriental lilies, but Mom made us apologize and she got over it. The usual players were Tom, Jay, my older sister Elizabeth, Ben, and I. Then there were other kids who would join us from further down Hancock and Adam Streets. Tom and Jay were the oldest, and they ruled at the game. They always had new strategies or rules; the rest of would protest but would ultimately go along.

Often, we would use the area near Parker Meadow right off the bike path as our playing ground. The lack of houses in the immediate vicinity gave us more freedom. Sometimes the ground was so soggy that it sploshed with each step, which, when I was the hunter, I found a dead giveaway. Dad had taught me that I needed to stand quietly in the woods and just listen. Like he used to do when he was in Viet Nam.

In the woods, everything is different. Even the light slants in a different way. The trees have long crooked arms reaching out into the shadows, the leaves rustle behind your back, and sometimes, even the birds were absent. If I sat really still for a long time, the birds and animals would just ignore me while they did their thing.

The woods can be scary. My dad always says you have to treat them with respect. One night late last spring, just before school was over, I was near the bike path, and I saw this THING coming down the path. It was curved over, muttering, and looked as if it had wings. Later, when I stopped running, I realized it was a person carrying a bamboo pole across its back with bags hanging from it. Anyway, I turned and fled, weaving blindly through the trees, whose branches reached out slashing me. Sheer terror gave me wings, but I felt certain that I was being pursued as the stiff northeast breeze rushed in and early fallen leaves skittered across the path. Was that my heart I heard pounding, or the stalker's feet behind me?

I was embarrassed later, when Tom and Jay materialized from the shadows. "Where are you going? We saw you running as if a monster was chasing you."

"Nah. I was just heading for home." Jay looked at me with this knowing smile. I wish Elizabeth were here. She would smile and toss her hair, and they would forget this.

"Yeah?" scoffed Tom. "Thought you were running from Mrs. Haggarty."

"Bottle lady? No way!" Mom had told me that Mrs. Haggarty prowled the town early in the morning, rescuing the recyclables and returning at least two bags of cans and bottles a day to the store. Probably she lived off the money, Mom pointed out. She was the reason why our recyclable basket never had any soda cans in it. It just had the regular cans and plastics. When I thought about it, she was doing Lexington a service. Mrs. Haggarty recycled all those cans that others tossed. She must collect many more than two bags a day.

"Probably she's on her way to the store with all her bottles."

Suddenly, Ben appeared. He's my age and Tom's younger brother. "What's going on?"

"Nothing," I said.

Jay pointed at me. "Tell the truth, Sam. You were running from Bottle Lady, weren't you?"

"Me? No way. Why should an ugly old woman make me run?"

"She's bad news. Have you ever seen her cats? UGLY!" exclaimed Tom.

"She's at least 100 years old; she lives in the house behind the pond—the one covered with bushes—and SHE hates kids," Jay said.

Ben and I looked at each other. I could see him thinking that they were just putting us on. Just because they were older, they always liked to appear like they knew everything.

"How do you know she hates kids?" I asked.

"Because she comes out of her house sometimes and yells at us."

"Yeah, she shakes her broom at us and calls us devils."

During the school year, we had homework so we had to wait to play flashlight tag until June when school was out. Mom let us stay out later at night, and we spent a lot of time strategizing our game. Sometimes Elizabeth was on our side; sometimes she sided with Tom and Jay because she was only a year younger than they were and two years older than Ben and me. I think Tom liked her anyway.

That first night after school was out, we all met downtown at the ice cream store.

Tom, Jay, and Elizabeth came up to Ben and me. "We've been thinking….that it would be more interesting if we put you two through initiation."

"No way," said Ben.

Ben never went along with anything, I thought. "What about Elizabeth?" I asked.

"She's older, so let's agree that she's already passed initiation."

"Unfair!"

"Hey, we make the rules here. And you're the one who wants to be an Airborne Ranger, right?" Jay smirked. "What's that song you sing? I wanna be an Airborne Ranger. I wanna lead a life of danger….right."

"Right," I growled.

"So we're giving you some danger so you two can prove yourselves." Tom smiled.

Great. I'll show them, I thought. My big problem will be Ben. Sometimes he wimped out on me.

"We're thinking that you should go to old lady Haggarty's house and get something to prove that you've been there."

"Have you ever done that?" Elizabeth asked. *Sometimes sisters come through,* I thought.

"Well, sometimes we think about it…" Jay and Tom looked at each other and laughed. "We dared each other to peer through her windows, but usually there are newspapers piled up in front of them."

Jay inserted, "She collects cans too. She has stacks of recyclables piled in the garage."

"They're all covered with fungus and stuff and smell like vomit. Then she has all these ratty-looking cats that are missing parts." Tom spat on the ground.

"Missing parts?" Ben's voice was higher than usual.

"Yeah, like legs or an ear or an eye. She even has one who just walks around in circles with his head tilted, meowing. My mother says he probably has a middle ear problem."

"And they live all over—like in her woodpile or the old tires she has piled on her grass."

" We thought to make it interesting … you have to get inside the house and bring out something."

"Like what?"

"The broom," Tom said. "You two bring the broom."

Ben and I looked at each other. This sounded hard, but I knew we were up to it. If I was going to be an Army Ranger when I grew up, I could certainly sneak into Bottle Lady's house. "First we need to reconnoiter, Ben. Let's check it out tomorrow."

Tom spoke up. "She always leaves the house very early—before the newspaper comes—looking for things in people's recycling. Then she goes home, and I don't know what happens after that."

"We'll find out," I said. "You can count on it." I thought that sounded like an Army Ranger. I almost said SIR.

The next day, Ben and I biked over to Mrs. Haggarty's. I had brought a flashlight, figuring if the windows were all covered by newspaper, the house would be dark. There was no sign that anyone was there; the downstairs windows were piled high with newspapers, but we couldn't see anyone in the upper windows. We walked furtively across the drive, trying not to crunch the gravel loudly. A skinny black cat with only three legs meowed at us. The wind moaned. Odd bits of horror movies that I had seen clawed at my mind.

The garage door was open. We poked our heads in. The smell was thick and fetid. It was like thick smoke, clinging to me. I wanted to puke. Jay was right. The recyclable bottles and cans were stacked up to the ceiling: Pepsi products along one wall, Coke along another, beer on the third. They were covered with thick velvety mold. Green plastic bags filled with half-gallon soda jugs stacked up on each other divided the room in half. She had enough recyclables here to feed her for the next five years! Flies were crawling all over. They were buzzing around my ears, biting me. We could hear a rat-like scuttling in the corner. A shaky tiger striped cat with mangy skin staggered in front of us and vomited strands of bloodstained mucus filled with glistening, writhing worms. YUCK! I thought of my healthy orange cat named Mick Jagger. What a contrast! Suddenly, a large rat scuttled across the floor. We jumped, knocking some cans over, and laughing with joy that we were leaving this place of horrors, we ran outside.

A yellow cat was standing by my bike, crying and scratching around. It was missing one eye and one ear flapped down. As I approached, it puffed up, locking eyes with me, staring without fear. Then it turned around and ran.

That night I asked mom what you could do to block bad smells. She said on one of her TV shows a detective disguised bad smells by dabbing some Vicks Vapor Rub under the nose. "That way," she said, "instead of smelling whatever it is you don't want to smell, you get the strong aroma of eucalyptus and menthol. If you want some, there's a jar in the medicine cabinet."

The next day we went back again—with two flashlights and a half-full jar of Vicks. We dabbed it under our noses and quickly walked through the garage to the inside door. I told myself that I would only open the door a crack, take a quick look, grab the broom, and close it. I put my hand on the knob and slowly turned it.

No broom was visible. All I could see was a narrow goat path of boxes and bundles of string-tied newspapers and magazines connecting the darkened rooms. A cat meowed overhead. A sweet dank smell drifted around me. Something rustled behind me; I turned quickly, but only Ben was there. Ben's cheeks were pale, his lips thin and trembling. A cat brushed my legs. I almost screamed. We stood there quietly, listening to a board creak above us. Despite the Vicks, I could still smell that smell. It was like 100 unemptied cat boxes. My eyes watered. Piles of liquid brown stuff lay on the floor—I didn't want to think what that was. "Where's the broom," I asked, spinning on my heel to inspect this nauseating place.

"I don't know. Let's give this up." He turned to leave. "Tom and Jay are jerks."

Silently, I agreed. Why was I here? But I didn't want to go home without the broom. I would never live that down. "Wait. Ben. We've got to prove to them that we can do this."

"Sure, sure." His hand was on the doorknob.

The smell was deep inside me now. I could barely breathe. "What's that?" I pointed to a mammoth lump further down the hall at the foot of the stairs. The broom lay next to it. "Go get it."

"No way, Jose. I'm not planning to be an Army Ranger. You do it."

I hated him. "Okay, okay. Give me the flashlight." I felt a tight knot in my stomach as I walked down the hall. The smell got worse. I could hear chewing noises—like Jagger made when I fed him—which wasn't often enough, according to Mom. A cat leapt away from the lump. Reaching down, I grabbed the broom, looking down at the lifeless lump. White gelatinous things were crawling on what appeared to be a face. *"Ohmygod,* Ben. It's her. "

"What?"

He didn't hear me. "I got the broom, Ben. Let's get out of here." Turning, we ran back into the garage, past all the cans and into the yard. We grabbed our bikes as another emaciated cat slunk away.

When I was home, I decided not to tell anyone what I saw lying on the floor. Ben and I would just give the others the broom and go on like normal. But I didn't feel like normal. I was sure that the permeating, nauseating smell was on my clothes and hair.

For a long time, I dreamed about Mrs. Haggarty's house. I only had to shut my eyes to see the mold reaching up to the ceiling with its thick velvet fingers or the maggots crawling on her face. She was found about two weeks later— neighbors had noticed the smell from the house and reported it.

One night at supper Mom said, "Somebody told me today that Mrs. Haggarty had about sixty cats at her place, and they're now all over the neighborhood scavenging for food and carrying diseases."

I held myself still, waiting, but that's all she said. When Elizabeth and I went to meet the others that night at the playing ground, I sensed a presence, watching us. The trees had hungry outstretched arms. Elizabeth took off with my flashlight. The moon shone on the meadow, where a three-legged cat leapt for the bushes. I forced myself to move, out across the damp grass, which squished underfoot. A cat yowled in the distance. I could hear someone or something breathing. Hopefully, it was Elizabeth. Army Rangers do just fine in the dark, I told myself. A cat meowed close by. Suddenly, a cat leapt in front of me. Startled, I backed up and fell over. That was when I saw all the skinny cats approaching.

Parker Meadow remains a ghost-filled area. The sun is reduced to pale shafts of light in this heavily wooded spot; the mist rises off the pond; and strange shapes flit from tree to tree. It is not a place to go alone at night.

Yankee Doodle Dandy

My name is John Howard. I'm one of the seven hundred British soldiers under the command of Lieutenant Colonel Francis Smith and, Marine Major John Pitcairn, who, on April 18, 1775, was ordered to destroy the military stores and supplies collected in Concord by the colonials.

What a horrendous assignment! First we had to cross the Charles River; then we had to wade through the East Cambridge swamps, where we got wet up to our knees; finally, we had to march, cold and wet, toward Lexington to arrest the rebel leaders, Samuel Adams and John Hancock. After that, we were to march to Concord and destroy the military supplies stored there. A relief column under the command of Lord Hugh Percy would leave several hours after the main column.

While Paul Revere and his cohorts were riding through the countryside, waking up all those colonials, we were slogging through cold, wet, smelly, marshy muck. We were tired, hungry, and wanted to get back to Boston.

I had thought being a grenadier would be a great adventure. So far it hadn't been. No one seems to know what to do, and few of my compatriots have ever experienced combat. As the second son, I had joined the military when I was finished with school. My older brother got the estate. Second brothers get the military or the ministry. I found the former more appealing. I've been here in the colonies as a soldier in his Majesty's 10th Regiment of Foot since the fall of 1774. Really, it has been quite dull—other than the Bostonians calling us Lobsterbacks or throwing a few snowballs. It's colder here than at home, and Boston has great falls of snow with hard winds. I wouldn't mind some action—but not when my feet are cold and wet, and I'm hungry and tired.

Lexington

As the sun came up, we marched with practiced precision into Lexington, a small farming town of about 800 people. We all felt awful, but we looked impressive. Our breeches were stained and dirty from the marshes, but our coats were brilliant red and our buckles shone in the rising sun. We were the most formidable fighting force of our era: red-uniformed precision, glitter, and polish. Probably a lot of those farmers had never seen a real British soldier—at least not like us. Bells rang out, and a drum was beating as we marched in unison down the street. Left, right, left, right.

We had heard some hundreds of people were collected together intending to oppose us, but there was only a group of ragtag farmers and shopkeepers standing on the Common, carrying their own weapons. They were barely in formation. One guy even had his powder and musket balls in his hat at his feet. A tallish fellow, who must have been their captain, stood out in the front. Some men were running out of the tavern, including two carrying a big trunk. Women and children were peering out from behind the several houses surrounding the Common.

We marched slowly in unison. Our backs were straight, our eyes to the right, we carried heavy knapsacks, and our bayonets were gleaming. Our drum beats and fife music filled the air. My friend, Harry, nudged me. "Is your musket loaded?"

"Of course," I retorted out of the side of my mouth. "I put so much powder in it that it will kick like a horse."

Harry snickered. "And you will have a bruised shoulder for sure. You don't think we will have to use our bayonets, do you?" A muscle twitched near the side of his mouth.

I licked my lips. My mouth was so dry.

"Maybe you will get to stick one of those Rebels," said Joseph on his other side.

Seemed to me that we were talking foolishness. We wouldn't be using our Brown Bess or bayonets. We would stand around like we did in Boston. The mob would call us names, and we would pretend that we hadn't heard them. We would be frozen faced, stiff lipped, and face them down one more time.

These colonials looked serious though. Some appeared far too old to be even contemplating firing their ancient muskets, and some looked younger than I. Dogs were barking, smoke was coming from some of the chimneys, and people were watching from the side. The sun was rising—ever so slowly.

Major Pitcairn rode his prancing horse towards the rebels. He was a huffy fellow, with massive contempt for farmers who thought they were soldiers. He roared, "Disperse! Lay down your arms, you damned rebels and disperse." Just the silence answered him. Again, red faced and determined, he yelled, "Why don't you disperse, you rebels? Disperse!" Again, only grim silence.

Wheeling his horse around, Pitcairn waved his sword and shouted to us, "Press forward, men." We marched past our drummers, wheeling and turning like we do on parade. We rotated to face the farmers—we had become a wall of red,

The Regulars advance—bayonets fixed. *Courtesy of Paul E. Doherty*

Yankee Doodle, Keep It Up

The origin of the word "Yankee" is unclear, but by the mid-1700s it referred to the English colonists, particularly New Englanders. British military officers sung "Yankee Doodle Dandy" before the Revolution to mock the "Yankees" with whom they served in the French and Indian War. A "dandy" is a British term for a man who spends his income on clothes in order to "appear above his station." A "doodle" was a country bumpkin.

Originally, "Yankee Doodle" was intended to deride the colonials:

> *Yankee Doodle came to town,*
> *For to buy a firelock;*
> *We will tar and feather him*
> *And so we will John Hancock.*
> *Yankee Doodle Dandy,*
> *Mind the music and the step,*
> *And with the girls be handy.*

Folklore says that the Yankees began to sing the song as they forced the British back to Boston on April 19, after the battles of Lexington and Concord.

facing these rebels with their floppy hats. Harry and Joseph looked shrunken and cold. Suddenly, I knew that this wasn't an exercise; it was something much worse.

Fortunately, their captain commanded his men to back off. As they slowly retreated, a single shot was fired. I don't know who fired it, but we fired several volleys, and then we charged those farmers—our bayonets fixed. Some even broke ranks to chase the colonials. The battle lasted only for several minutes because a purple-faced Major Pitcairn was screaming at us to stop firing. When we did, seven rebels lay dead and one was crawling across the Common. They looked like rag dolls. I saw one with a ragged hole in his cheek, blood pouring down his neck. Another was staggering along, holding his stomach with bloody red hands until two of our soldiers bayoneted him in the back. The sun was up; the grass was red; and we had just killed eight men on an April morning.

They were just like us, but now in a twinkling of an eye, they were dead. Just like that: Life was over for these men who were British—just like I am. Then, our fifes began to play, and our drums beat the cadence. We fired a salute, gave three loud huzzahs, stepped over the rebel bodies, and resumed our march to Concord.

I had seen action, but I'm not sure I liked it.

Concord

We marched another five miles to Concord, where we were supposed to destroy a magazine and stores collected there. The sun was up, and we had been up the whole night. Lieutenant Colonial Smith divided our force. He sent seven light infantry companies to the North Bridge, one to guard the South Bridge, and deployed the others in town, where they searched for military stores. I was in the latter group. I was hoping to find some food and a place to sleep, but that wasn't to be.

We found little in the way of munitions. Our spy had told us that the colonials hid their supplies in a Colonel Barrett's farm and mill, but we couldn't find them. To punish the defiant colonists, we chopped down their liberty pole and burned it and added some wooden gun carriages to the fire, making a lot of black smoke. But then the flames spread to the Town House, setting its roof on fire. Some women came rushing out, begging for our help to extinguish the fire. Despite what had happened in Lexington, we were all British. These people were our relatives, in a manner of speaking. So Harry and Joseph looked at me, and we formed a bucket brigade with the women. We saved the building. We all grinned happily at each other in our unexpected comradeship.

At the center of Concord on Lexington Road, Wright Tavern is a historic tavern located in the center of Concord, Massachusetts. It is now a National Historic Landmark. Wright Tavern was the headquarters of the Minutemen in the early morning of April 19, 1775. Later that day, the British companies regrouped at Wright Tavern and even rested for several hours (they had been up all night) before they began the long march back to Boston around noon. *Courtesy of Paul E. Doherty*

We met our fellow soldiers back at a tavern. Covered with dust, they looked like they had been running. I asked Ian, whom I knew from school, what had happened. His face was tense, "When we got there, we could see all these colonials across the bridge on a field. Some Regulars marched off in the direction of a farm. Others remained to guard the river crossing." He swallowed hard. "We could see the smoke from town. Several British companies were at the east end of the bridge. They were one behind the other so only the front company could fire without fear of harming one of our own. It was really narrow. To the north, we could see other regiments gathering."

His friend George interrupted him. "Then the senior rebel officer ordered the Yankees into a long line facing the bridge into the town. They began to march onto the bridge. Our Regulars began ripping up the planks to halt their advance, but then one of ours fired a warning shot. Others joined him, killing two and wounding several rebels."

Ian interrupted. "And this damn Yankee captain shouted, 'Fire, fellow soldiers, for God's sake, fire.' He shouldn't have done that. If he hadn't done that, then none of this would have happened."

"They didn't shoot anyone, did they?"

"Oh yes, they did. Those shabby farmers killed three of our regulars and wounded four officers." Ian spat with disgust. "Despite their scruffy appearance, they know how to use their weapons."

"So what happened next?"

"When our soldiers saw that the colonials were shooting and some of ours were going down, they began to fall back."

"They did?" I was stunned. British soldiers don't fall back.

"Well, we didn't think they were going to fire. We were just there to get those munitions. I wasn't more than twenty feet from one rebel when he threw up his musket and fired. He just missed me."

"You retreated?"

"I had to. They were shooting at us with their old muskets. I saw some of our guys fall! Some broke ranks, running toward town and even abandoning the wounded. I've never seen that before."

This was no longer an adventure. It was getting serious.

We ate, drank, and tended to our wounded. The rumor was that Colonel Smith and Major Pitcairn sat at the tavern stirring their drinks and vowing to stir Yankee blood that day. We could hear church bells in the distance: I wondered how long this day would be.

The Battle Road

At first, all was quiet as we wearily retreated from Concord, although we could see the colonial forces in the fields paralleling our line of march—rather frightening to know that we had a sixteen-mile journey back to Boston and safety, and they were all watching us.

The Concord River is only about fifteen miles long, but it has figured in history, literature, and many romances. North Bridge is where the colonials first resisted the British with signified force. Visitors can cross the reconstructed bridge and see Daniel Chester French's Minute Man statue. The North Bridge Visitor Center is at 174 Liberty Street, Concord. *Courtesy of Paul E. Doherty*

We were marching down the road when we came to a narrow bridge crossing a small brook. In the fields were what looked like hundreds of rebels. We jammed together as we crossed the bridge. We marched without music or a word being spoken. Suddenly, they fired. The balls were plowing up the road in front of us. Trees were cracking overhead from the fire, and dust flew everywhere. On the side of the road lay a grenadier. His white wig had fallen off his balding head. His blood had soaked the ground. He looked so young, even though he was balding. I wondered if he had joined to have an adventure, too.

The crooked road from Concord to Lexington was full of hills. The Yankees used the woods, thickets, and stonewalls to their advantage. Concealed behind them, they fired upon us constantly. Some rebels crawled up on my left flank. Cocking my musket, I saw the spurt of blood before I heard it blast. The colonial behind the first was splattered with brain matter. The first soldier had a flap of scalp jutting out behind his ear.

Then his body went limp, and he melted into the grass. I had shot someone. My legs turned to rubber. I was feeling dizzy. My uniform was covered with dust, and the sun was blazing. Suddenly, I vomited. Harry grabbed me. "Come on John. We're going to get out of here." We moved faster.

Further down the road were three dead Regulars. Some others, who were wounded, sat with them. One was begging for water; another cursing. Joseph, who was marching with his bayonet fixed, suddenly staggered; he had taken a musket ball in his neck. He went down. I singled out the rebel, whom I thought had attacked him, and took aim directly between his shoulders. Then I stopped; someone could be aiming at me right now, and I would die on this bloodstained road.

Harry grabbed me. "I heard that these provincials scalped a Regular back at the bridge. We've got to move faster."

The Yankees subjected us to the most grueling and deadly fire. As we passed one tavern, a grenadier was shot and fell. We shot madly into the upper story but with little effect. Another grenadier died down the road. Confusion increased. We were shot at, set upon, harassed, and killed. The Yankees set up ambushes from behind stonewalls, rocks, and orchards; they advanced, covered, and retreated. The fighting grew in intensity. A foot soldier near me grabbed for his throat. A red river gushed down past his collar. His mouth opened, but he made no sound. We marched slowly and steadily, but our column kept jerking to a stop as we needed to reload. When it moved again, more crumpled bodies lay on the road.

Harry looked exhausted. His face was gray and grimy; his eyes were red with fatigue and smoke. His buckles no longer glittered. I probably looked the same. In front of him, two Regulars staggered, trailing blood behind them as they tried to march down that long long road. We were covered with dust in beastly heat. An officer came dashing down the road on his beautiful horse. From the right flank, a rifle rang out. The horse reared, throwing the officer, who resembled a sack of corn. By the time we reached a tavern, thousands of colonials

Located within the Minuteman National Historical Park, the Hartwell Tavern was once a prosperous farm and tavern belonging to Ephraim and Elizabeth Hartwell. From the tavern, the Hartwells could see the British soldiers marching to Concord and retreating to Boston. Today, Hartwell Tavern is a "living history" center. Park rangers and volunteers dressed in period clothing demonstrate colonial activities and provide insight into colonial life. *Courtesy of Paul E. Doherty*

were unleashing incessant fire. They were everywhere—crawling on their bellies in the open meadows, lurking behind the stonewalls, hedges, and trees—firing, loading, firing again.

We jammed the road as we frantically retreated through the long warm day. An officer on horseback with a drawn sword attempted to rally us on a hill coming into Lexington. He rode back and forth, commanding and urging us on. Some rebels fired, the officer fell, and the horse ran directly toward the colonials. Harry gasped, grabbed his chest, and fell over on the road. I left him for the wagons and fled the hill with the colonials waving their guns in hot pursuit.

I couldn't believe it. He was my best friend, but I just left him.

I saw a small farmhouse and ran for it. There had to be some food and water. I spied the well and met a colonial. I drew up my musket, exclaiming, "You are a dead man."

"And so are you," he retorted.

We both fired, and we both fell. I died immediately. And he died the next day.

Our great adventure was over while America's was just beginning.

> *For decades, people have murmured about the haunts of Fiske Hill. Maybe the shadowy figures we see on those April spring days are why the teenagers never party on the hill. For two young men died there—just as they were beginning their lives.*

Postcard courtesy of S. L. Doran; S. Lawrence Whipple, collector

Historic Fiske Hill

Fiske Hill is part of the 750-acre Minuteman National Historical Park. If you walk east across the parking lot at the intersection of Route 2A and Old Massachusetts Avenue into the meadow, you see a small sign indicating the tree-lined path up the hill. At the top, a lovely open field greets you. When you descend the hill, you find the remains of the foundation of the Ebenezer Fiske House (1674), which was razed in 1955. This was the farmhouse where the British soldier entered. James Hayward of Acton went to the well. As the latter lay dying, he called for his powder horn and bullet pouch, remarking that he had started with one pound of powder and forty bullets. "You see what I have been about," he exclaimed, calling attention to the very little powder and two or three balls that he had left. "I am not sorry. I die willingly for my country."

The retreating British column left some wounded behind here, and Dr. Joseph Fiske, Ebenezer's cousin, treated them in the parlor of the house. Despite his efforts, the soldiers died and were buried on the property.

Erin Go Braugh

The gypsy rover came over the hill
Down through the valley so shady,
He whistled and he sang 'til the greenwoods rang,
And he won the heart of a lady.

Chorus:
Ah-de-do, ah-de-do-da-day,
Ah-de-do, ah-de-da-ay
He whistled and he sang 'til the greenwoods rang,
And he won the heart of a lady.

She left her father's castle gates
She left her own fine lover
She left her servants and her state
To follow the gypsy rover.

Her father saddled up his fastest steed
And roamed the valleys all over
Sought his daughter at great speed
And the whistling gypsy rover.

He came at last to a mansion fine,
Down by the river Claydee
And there was music and there was wine,
For the gypsy and his lady.

"He is no gypsy, my father" she said
"But lord of these lands all over,
And I shall stay 'til my dying day
With my whistling gypsy rover.

t took me all summer to convince Tom that we should buy the antique house at 20 Hancock Street. He scoffed at me, "That's no antique. It's just decrepit."

I counter-attacked with how charming the front and back stairs, window seats, and long Victorian windows were. He groaned that the rooms were small and the bathrooms miniscule. I pointed out that the house was built before the advent of bathrooms. "Think all those bedrooms had those lovely pitchers and bowls like we see in the antique stores?"

He laughed. "More likely, the house had an outhouse. Every penny we have will go into keeping it afloat."

"I'll go to work."

He didn't seem to hear me. "Not a day will go by," he thundered, "that something won't be leaking, cracking, peeling, falling down, or stopping up."

So I played my trump card: the guilt one. "We need a bigger house so we can move in your mother."

"You're right," he sighed. "I hate her being in New York by herself, climbing all those stairs."

"Aha, at last we agree on something. You're absolutely right."

He smiled. I continued. "She is getting to the place in life where she needs someone to care for her, and we're her only family."

He sighed again. "Okay, Okay. Let's do it."

Helen had emigrated from Ireland at age nineteen after the bloodthirsty Black and Tans had led her brothers out to dig their own graves during the Easter Rising. She had an eighth grade education and a great faith in the afterlife, having had little happiness in reality. "Oh," she would say, "life here is nothing but a vale of tears, but then when you get to the other side," and she would point up to the sky, "you will meet the dear Lord Jesus."

Her son, my husband Tom, was a PhD geophysicist. She talked about the dear Lord Jesus, and he quoted Einstein. She and I had more in common because we were two women, although she would often refer to me as "the little black Protestant who had saved her son from bachelorhood and brought her some dear little grandchildren."

Helen lived her life as if she expected to die the next day. One of her favorite phrases was, "I won't make old bones, you know." Each year at Christmas, she would rewrap the sweater, the afghan, etc. that we so carefully selected, hand it back to us, saying in her finest brogue, "I'll be dying this year, so you might as well return this."

One Christmas evening, Tom turned to me, saying, "Sometimes I understand why my father was an alcoholic. He was driven to the drink!"

Helen taught me about things I had never known growing up in a Connecticut suburb. She talked about the Black and Tans, the soldiers brought into Ireland by the government in London after 1918 to put down the Irish rebellion. I learned about the potato famine; the Sinn Fein; and the dreaded English; how to make Irish soda bread and colcannon; that it was bad luck to put shoes on a table or chair, place a bed facing the door, bring lilac into the house, cut your fingernails on Sunday, or give a knife as a gift.

I was positive (but then I was only twenty-eight years old) that we would all live happily ever after. The old house on Hancock Street would be a good investment, although I was one of the very few people who found it charming. Tom thought I was crazy, and many of my friends expressed their dismay. "Why do you want that house?" they asked. "It's such a mess." And it was. The former owners—despite having inscribed their great love for each other in the terrace cement—had divorced and left as soon as they received our down payment, abandoning their wedding pictures, toothbrushes, collections of *Penthouse* and *Playboy*, and their children's traffic violations. We spent many weekends there, cleaning out the remnants of their lives. Helen commented, "It's a dirty bird that won't keep its own nest clean."

Tom may have muttered about old houses, but he did remove one wall in the kitchen and added a bathroom upstairs.

Together, we scraped, sanded, painted, and papered. Although the former owners had told us there were no gardens, we found pink phlox, blue balloon flower, and snowy white Artemisia under piles of rotting leaves. To one side, we found an enormous pink peony bed. Large showy rhododendron stood in front of the house, and an old apple tree shaded the terrace. At the far end of the property stood great colonies of yellow iris. Pheasants paraded past, and we had flocks of birds.

Six-year old Siobhan and five-year-old Steve ran up the front stairs to the third floor and then down the back stairs. The clump clump of their steps echoed through the house, and Tom and I spoke hastily about procuring sound-muffling carpeting. Helen made tea and sat marveling at the many birds. "It's like rising in Ballighan and seeing the sun rise over the mountains." The old house stood straighter, glorying in its renovation and refurbishment.

After we moved in, neighbors dropped by with jars of jam and loaves of banana bread. Our children played, as we had coffee or lunched. Unfortunately, several of my new friends were British, which upset Helen when she heard their clipped English accents. That night she told the children that the neighbors "were guilty of sin—a sin which cries to the Holy Ghost for vengeance." Siobhan burst into tears and came running to us. Long talks and a bowl of popcorn later, she had calmed down.

Tom and I looked at each other. "Okay, who's going to talk to your mother?" I asked, feeling frustrated.

"You'd be better." *Honestly, men,* I thought as I went to Helen's room. She too was shaking and trembling, muttering that the Black and Tans were coming to get her. Her cheeks were pale, her lips trembling, her eyes haunted. "They're right outside the door," she sobbed. I reassured her that we were in America, and that the Black and Tans were terrorists from the past.

She sighed, "They'll never be in the past for me. I don't want you to be friends with those people."

"Why?"

"They're British. And it's like they say, *he who lies down with the dogs will rise up with the fleas.*"

"But Helen…"

She interrupted me. "Hush. *Nobody knows where his sod of death is.*"

That type of statement kills conversation as far as I am concerned, so I shut my mouth. Tom and I decided that instead of my playing the freelance editor at home and becoming friends with people with English accents that I would return to full-time work. I had talked about doing that anyway, so it was a happy compromise for all concerned.

I went to work; the children were in camp; and Helen stayed home. She puttered about the kitchen, emptied the dishwasher, and folded laundry. Slowly, she discarded her ancient black silk dresses and black stockings that were suitable, maybe to New York City, and wore simpler clothes. She seemed happier, although she still talked about when she would join the dear Lord Jesus, which puzzled the kids. "Why does Granny want to die?" asked Siobhan. "Doesn't she like being with us?"

The produce from our vegetable garden put an end to her death wish. I would leave her to skin and peel tomatoes and then can them when I came home. We would find Helen touching the filled Mason jars, talking about how good it would be in the winter. Tom and I began to buy cases of fruit from the orchards. She would peel and core twenty pounds of apples during the day; then I would make applesauce when I came home. We ate a lot of applesauce in those days. The pantry closet filled up with jars of peaches, pears, applesauce, and tomatoes. We would find Helen standing in front of the open closet, reverently touching the jars, muttering about how she had to stay alive so she could eat all of the dear Lord's bounty.

Helen began to smile more often. She stopped talking about the dear Lord Jesus waiting for her. One day, she told me that she heard someone singing *Too-ra-loo-ra-loo-ral* in the house. I looked at her blankly, and she said, "That's an Irish lullaby, don't you know." Then she shuffled off singing, "Too-ra-loo-ra-loo-ral, Too-ra-loo-ra-loo-ral, Hush, now don't you cry!" She started darning Tom's socks and sewed buttons back on. She polished the brass and shined silver. She told the kids stories about pirates and how they kidnapped St. Patrick and sold him into slavery in Ireland. That story alone was good for several weeks of playacting. Life was good.

One night, Helen was telling us about Ireland in the old days when her father was the groundskeeper on this big estate owned by an English gentleman. Suddenly, our front door opened wide, bringing a whiff of pipe tobacco with it, and then slowly closed again. She smiled gently and said, "It must be the Irishman."

"Who's that?" asked Siobhan, terrified.

Helen looked confused and then said, "Oh, I meant to say it was the leprechauns. They're out playing tricks tonight."

We laughed, but I wondered why I smelled pipe tobacco.

Helen's room was at the back of the house, overlooking the garden. When the weather was good, she would sit outside enjoying the birds and the flower gardens we had planted. We built her a small porch off the kitchen so she didn't have to go down the stairs. She never left the house anymore. I did her shopping, and church was no longer important to her. Her life was winding down. "Everything I want is right here, dear."

"You sure?"

"Oh yes... Sometimes I see the blessed Virgin all in white and raising her hands and eyes to heaven with a hovering lamb sitting right over the garden. That's when I pray." I figured if the apparition made her happy, why should I worry?

Some days I thought I heard her talking, but she was alone when I looked into her room. She was smiling at the opposite wall. I asked what she was looking at. She blinked at me, "Oh nothing. Old age is hard enough, but when the eyesight begins to dim, the good Lord is laying a heavy burden on my poor frail self." When I left, she was smiling and talking again.

One Saturday morning at breakfast, she told us that there was an old cistern in the garden, under one of the peonies. In it, she said, was lovely old glassware from the seventeen hundreds. Tom said, "Sure, Mom, and I have other things to do. Like mowing the lawn."

Steve looked up from his Legos, "Is this like a treasure hunt?"

"I guess it can be," I replied, "but let me dig up the peony first. It's October, and I can divide it now anyway." The kids and I dug, until we found the old cistern. In the bottom were lovely small blue glass bottles—probably used by an old colonial, I thought.

When we showed our treasure to Tom, he frowned, "How did Mom know it was there?"

"Maybe she has second sight. She *is* Irish after all." He laughed, and the day went on with all its demands and interruptions until we forgot about it.

One Saturday, the grandchildren of the former owners stopped by. Older than we were, they told us more of the history of the house. Their ancestors had been two sisters, who were the seamstresses of Lexington, designing, fabricating, and sewing debutante and wedding dresses in what we called the walk-through room on the second floor. They each had a family and had divided the front, saltbox portion of the house between them. They were the ones who had planted the pink peonies in the lower garden in 1913.

Helen asked them about the Irishman. They shook their heads, looking confused. What Irishman? They didn't know anything about the Irishman. She insisted that an Irishman had owned the house.

"He's here," she repeated stubbornly.

Tom interrupted, "Mother! The Irish weren't liked here. There were signs up in those days saying, "No Irish need apply."

"No, son, he was long before that. He came in the early 1800s to dig the railroad."

A week later, I was awakened in the middle of the night by someone singing, singing, " Too-ra-loo-ra-loo-ral, Too-ra-loo-ra-loo-ral, Hush, now don't you cry!" Then Helen came into our room. She was fully dressed. A good-looking young man stood next to her. "Helen," I gasped, "Is everything all right?"

She patted my hand, "I'm just fine, dear," grabbed the hand of the young man, and left. I sat up, thinking what a weird dream. Nothing moved in the room. The house was quiet. I got up and went to Helen's room. The moon was shining in the window. Helen was lying in her bed, in her neatly-buttoned pink flannel nightgown, dead. She had a lovely smile on her face.

Several weeks later, during one of those late fall storms, I was closing the windows before the rain came when I heard someone singing, "Too-ra-loo-ra-loo-ral, Too-ra-loo-ra-loo-ral, Hush, now don't you cry." The song seemed to come from Helen's room. When I looked in there, I smelled the whiff of pipe tobacco. As I stood sniffing, two shadows glided past me, pale in the dim light. They were holding hands as they disappeared into the watery light.

Voices from the Past

My brother, Karl Theodor Christian Friedrich Follen, and I were educated at the preparatory school at Giessen, Germany, where he distinguished himself for proficiency in Greek, Latin, Hebrew, French, and Italian. And I ... well, I distinguished myself in nothing as my father pointed out—quite loudly. When Karl was seventeen, he entered the University of Giessen. In 1814, the two of us fought in the Napoleonic Wars as Hessian volunteers. We returned home, having ended French domination, to find that we still faced university restrictions and aristocratic rule in our own country! Redrawing Europe's map after Napoleon's defeat, the Congress of Vienna had chosen absolute monarchy and stability over civil liberties and national unification of the German nation.

Now, Karl was very idealistic. He found the situation intolerable and noisily expressed his displeasure. Not only was he involved in organizing revolutionary student organizations, such as the *Burschenschaften*, he was loudly agitating for reform. His essays and speeches advocated violence and death to all tyrants. He looked the part: He and his group members wore their hair long, sported black velvet coats, and carried knives. Karl supported a unified Germany and called for the overthrow of the government, by force, if necessary.

We marched, chanted, and called for nationalism. Karl, who was studying law, joined a radical fraternity, and wrote political essays, poems, and patriotic songs. When the university outlawed the fraternity, Karl called for revolutionary upheaval.

In the midst of this chaos, he earned his degree of doctor of civil law in 1817 and moved to Jena, where he became a lecturer at the University. Karl's radicalism culminated in his support of a student, Carl Ludwig Sand, who in 1819, killed the Russophile diplomat and dramatist August von Kotzebue, who had publicly ridiculed the students' ideas in his weekly publication. Karl was so committed to violence in the name of freedom that he was labeled "the German Robespierre." Government surveillance and crackdown increased. Karl returned to Giessen, where he soon incurred the wrath of the government because of his liberal political ideas. I had already been jailed for circulating a petition begging for the introduction of a representative government. Recognizing that he was in danger, Karl fled Germany for Paris, where he met the Marquis de Lafayette.

In France, he came under suspicion again after Charles Ferdinand, duc de Berry, was assassinated in 1820, so he fled to Zurich, Switzerland. There he became professor of Latin in the cantonal school of the Grisons and then a civil law professor at the University of Basel. His revolutionary past caught up with him, however, and he was exiled from Germany and then Switzerland.

Coming to America

Fearful for his freedom, the twenty-eight-year-old Karl came to the United States. Anglicizing his name to Charles, he perfected his English and became a citizen. With letters of introduction from the Marquis de Lafayette, he established himself in Massachusetts' society. He became a teacher at the Round Hill School in Northampton, Massachusetts, and married Eliza Lee Cabot—one of the Boston Cabots—in 1828, thus assuring his place in society. Although he gradually became American, he retained his passionate commitment to political and social reform.

In 1829, Charles was appointed an instructor of German at Harvard. New Englanders had little knowledge of the German language or culture, and almost no German books were available at Harvard or in the Boston bookstores. Charles had to develop his own textbooks. He wrote a German Reader for Beginners and a German Grammar, which have been college textbooks for several generations. He was also charged with setting up the first gymnastics program at the College on the Delta, where Memorial Hall now stands.

Although the financially powerful Boston merchants tended to be socially conservative, the city had its political, social, and religious reformers who had a strong sense of responsibility for the community at large. Charles became friendly with the New England Transcendentalists, introducing them to a more systematic approach and German Romantic thought. Through Eliza, he became acquainted with Boston's most prominent figures. Everyone knew my charming, intelligent brother. One day, he met William Ellery Channing, a leading Unitarian minister, who encouraged him to study for the ministry. Soon Charles embarked on a preaching career in addition to his duties at Harvard. Unlike myself, Charles was very gifted. He could speak so persuasively that others would do his bidding. He was bright and engaging; I could have been very envious—except that he had a fatal flaw. Each time, just as his life was becoming really good, he always went just one step too far. A visionary, he never learned when to back off.

By 1830, my brother was the father of one child and a homeowner on a Cambridge street that is now known as Follen Street. There, according to many, he introduced the decorated Christmas tree, a German custom, to puritanical New England. Happiness reigned. During this period, many of the merchants who supported the churches in Boston profited either from the infamous Triangle Trade or from slave-grown goods such as cotton cloth, rum, etc. They saw abolition as a threat to their wealth and the social order, while Charles, a true social reformer, gravitated to it.

The 1820s and 1830s were years of friction and change between the Harvard student body and the administration. By 1834, Charles was approaching the equivalent of tenure at Harvard. He also was a committed, uncompromising abolitionist, admired by other abolitionists and despised by slaveholders. Despite the recommendations of his Harvard colleagues to avoid the movement, he had befriended abolitionist William Lloyd Garrison, helped found the Cambridge Anti-Slavery

Society at Harvard, and had become an active member and officer of the New England Anti-Slavery Society

After nearly ten years of teaching, Charles' outspoken abolitionist beliefs and his opposition to the disciplinary measures that President Josiah Quincy imposed on undergraduates led to his dismissal from Harvard. Recovering from this blow, he became ordained as a Unitarian minister in 1836. He took a pulpit at All Souls Church in New York City, where, once again, he alienated the congregation with his abolitionism. This series of professional disasters led to grave financial problems.

Coming to Lexington

During the early nineteenth century, Lexington was a small village with three great roads: Concord and Middlesex Turnpikes and Old Concord Road. Horse- and oxen-drawn wagons traveled those roads, carrying produce from Vermont and New Hampshire farms to Boston and returning with cotton, silk, needles, and other luxuries from abroad. Cattle and swine went through town to the Brighton cattle market. As in most New England towns, the meetinghouse was the focal point of social, political, and religious life for the citizens.

The early nineteenth century saw the birth of the lyceum movement with its focus on lifelong education. People in those days enjoyed listening to lectures and sermons—in the same way that we attend adult education classes today. They wanted their understanding to be broadened, their imagination to be stimulated, and their emotions aroused.

This century was also the time of the Second Great Awakening, which was stimulated by new religious thought, and the separation of church and state in Massachusetts in 1833. Great Awakenings often see the rise of new denominations and changes in religious thought, which often become part of the nation's political platforms. For example, the abolition movement, part of the wider Second Great Awakening, contributed to the American Civil War.

This view of Massachusetts Avenue in East Lexington shows (from left to right) the Follen Church, the Stone Building, a house, and a store.

In 1830, a public-minded Lexingtonian, Eli Robbins, erected a three-story observatory on the highest point in town. Many carriages drove on weekends to see Boston Harbor from that vantage point and to visit with the neighbors. By 1833, Robbins, who shared a deep commitment to equality and anti-slavery with Charles, decided to construct a public building where lectures, preaching, and other meetings could be held and where freedom of speech could be allowed. He intended this building, which is now known as the East Branch Library or the Stone Building, to be built as a free and open meetinghouse, intending it for abolitionist speakers who were not permitted to speak elsewhere in town. Several years passed before any public anti-slavery speech, besides the Follen Church sermons, were presented there, however.

In 1833, approximately 300 people lived in Lexington's East Village. Dense woods—and a long two-mile trip in those horse-and-buggy days—separated them from the center part of town. Consequently, they asked town authorities to provide a church and minister since the main meetinghouse was such a distance! When they were unsuccessful, the East Villagers formed the

Religious Society of East Village and began meeting in Robbin's handsome Greek revival hall. They asked Charles to preach in this hall and assist them in forming a society. In 1839, they asked him to minister to their congregation. My brother had finally found a congregation who wanted him and his ideas!

Unfortunately, the salary was not large, and Charles had to earn extra income by lecturing. Still he encouraged the women of the church to hold a fair to aid in completing and furnishing the church. He then prepared the plan for the octagonal church, which still stands as the oldest church in Lexington. He wanted the church to be a fine specimen of art in its design and proportions—to be a beautiful though simple model for other churches. His design had the minister being one with the parishioners—not being elevated above them.

In January 1840, Charles was earning extra money by lecturing in New York City. On his way home from New York for the dedication of the East Lexington church, my brother was killed in a fire on board the steamship *Lexington*. He was forty-four years old. The Anti-slavery Society made arrangements to hold a public memorial service, but because he was an abolitionist, no church wanted to hold his service—even his own church, which he had designed! Finally, the outspoken abolitionist Samuel May conducted the memorial service at Marlborough Chapel in Boston on April 17, 1840.

Leaving a Legacy

During the winter of 1846-47, some of the ablest speakers of their time gave a series of lectures at Robbin's hall. The speakers included Charles Sumner, Wendell Phillips, Theodore Parker, and Josiah Quincy Jr.

Ultimately, Robbin's hall, which had witnessed some of the most powerful orators of that period, became a family home. Abner Stone bought the Greek Revival building at 735 Massachusetts Avenue in 1851. The classically beautiful building played many roles over the years. Several schools operated within; it served as a private honeymoon suite; but in 1891, it found a new role.

Miss Ellen A. Stone gave it to the town to use as a library, reading room, and for other purposes. In accepting the gift, the town voted to call the building the "Stone Building." It remained a library until 2006, when a flood damaged it. Today, the town is debating how to restore and utilize this historic hall.

> *For several years, people have said that the Stone Building has a ghost who wanders its rooms. Some say the ghost is a former librarian, but perhaps it is Charles Follen who is still proclaiming the need for freedom for all. Maybe he wonders why the church he designed refused to hold his memorial service. Maybe he is still looking for a place where he is fully accepted. Perhaps the closest he came to being accepted was here in Lexington.*

Weaver's Song

Weaver's life is like an engine,
Coming around the mountain steep,
Had our ups and downs a-plenty
And at night we cannot sleep.

—The Weaver's Song
(trad. late 1800s-early 1900s)

When I told my mama that I wanted to leave my home on the farm and go to Concord to work in the mill, she shook her head. "You can't leave the farm, Helen. We need you here. Who's going to collect all those eggs? Feed the cows?"

"I don't know, mama, but I'm nineteen years old. I want to see the world. *And I hate those chickens,* I thought.

She looked down at the bowl of peas that she was shelling. "Working in a mill can be dangerous!"

"Some may say that, but think, Mama, I get a chance to be on my own. You always said that you regretted that you never went anywhere or did anything other than be a farmer's wife."

"True, but I'll worry about you."

"But, Mama, I can do it. I promise I will be safe. Besides, I will make some money. The recruiter told me that because there are so many mills in the area I could earn a good deal—more than I could anywhere else around. Almost $2 a week, he said."

"That's good money. You will need to work hard, but you know that hard work is no disgrace." She looked down at her tired reddened hands.

"I will send you some money each month. I promise." I had to get away. This was my big chance. If I wanted to get married, I needed to save something in the way of a dowry. But first I needed to meet a few men, which I certainly wasn't going to do while sitting on this farm taking care of those fool chickens.

She put the bowl of peas down. "I've learned that the only way you are going to get anywhere in life is to work hard at it and to believe in yourself. If you remain blessed with your health, you will probably do better there than you could here." I knew she was right. Marrying a farmer is serious business. You get so exhausted from raising crops and livestock, cooking, cleaning, having babies, nursing the sick, and making clothing, soap, and candles.

People must have laughed when I got out of the coach in Concord, dressed in my homespun dress with a shawl pinned under my chin covering my head. I had a small trunk covered with the skin of brown and white calves, containing all my worldly possessions.

I got a room at the boardinghouse connected with the mill. The widow who was running it stated firmly, "My name is Mrs. Jane. You will call me that. I have kept a boardinghouse for eight years. There has been death in my house; three have gone home sick, two have been dismissed for bad conduct."

"Yes, ma'm."

"The doors are LOCKED at ten pm. And I expect you to attend church services."

I nodded. "Yes, Mrs. Jane."

"My duty is to serve you and the others good solid meals on time and to be sure that the boarders maintain good order. If you don't…"

"I will, ma'm."

"No cursing or staying out after curfew." She glanced at me, "I take it you are a Yankee."

"Yes, ma'm."

"That's good. I am putting you with Sally. We always make roommates take care of each other. She will take you to the mill and introduce you to the overseers and counting room folks."

The boardinghouse was crowded with beds, bandboxes and trunks, and people. The first floor contained a kitchen, dining room, and Mrs. Jane's quarters. There were thirty-six girls in the six upstairs bedrooms. We slept two in a bed, three beds in a room. We used our trunks as desks and bureaus. It was weird to climb into bed and feel the shape in the hair mattress of the last girl who stayed here at Mrs. Jane's. I fit perfectly into her hollow on the sagging old bed.

On my first day at the mill—which seemed enormous—Sally ushered me into the ground floor counting room next to the entrance gate. The clerk wrote down my name in his leather bound book, where I was born, my local address, and the date of my entry into the mill work force. Next to this, he wrote down *new*.

He looked up at me with his beady little eyes and said. "You must attend assiduously to your work during work hours. You must complete the work you have been given."

I nodded. He continued. "You must appear full of a praiseworthy love of temperance and virtue. You must attend public worship and may not be addicted to gambling." I wasn't quite sure what that meant, but I nodded anyway. He continued, "Remember more and more people are coming here, and they will want your job if you don't."

"Oh sir, I want it."

"There will be no spirits and no games of chance. You will stay here for at least a year."

"Yes, sir."

"You are in the weaving department. You will work alongside Abigail; she's an old timer. You will get $2 a week in addition to a small charge for your housing and meals." I would put my wages into the savings bank until I sent some of it home, I thought. My parents could use something to help make ends meet.

The weaving department was where the production of cloth actually began. Before the cotton got there, workers had separated, straightened, and twisted cotton fibers and combined them into yarn. There were spindles, spinning frames, looms, spinning mules, spoolers, warpers, lappers and pickers, dressers, dressing frames, speeders, and stretchers. The overseers were responsible for us and looked after our interests. The spacious brick building had large whitewashed rooms. The noise was horrific. When I left that first night, my ears still heard the machines. The rhythm of my life in the factory was very different from that of the farm. The machines were a lot noisier, and the dust and lint made it hard to breathe,

The Damon Mill contains offices today, but for several centuries it was associated with industry and manufacturing. The Assabet River supplied the power to keep the mill wheels turning and the water necessary for processing.*Courtesy of D. Peter Lund*

but $2 a week was enough to purchase any essentials, maybe send some money back home, and build up my savings account.

That goal gave me the impetus to go back the next day and learn from Abigail how to thread the shuttles and tie weaver's knots. At first the days seemed endless. When I left at night, I was covered with white dust from the lint, and my ears still heard the sound of the mill. My feet ached, and my ankles were white and puffy from standing so much.

After two months, when a regular operative left, however, I was good enough to work two looms. I also was handling my new spending money quite happily.

Boardinghouse life was really fun. After we cleared the cake, pie, and biscuit with its "sauce" from the supper table, some of us would bring our sewing and diaries to the table. There we would sit and talk. Sometimes someone would read a letter from home or share a present that had been sent. Sometimes we would read the Bible, *Pilgrim's Progress*, or Sunday school books. Usually, we just talked, sharing our hopes and dreams. Some of the other girls went to their rooms; some went for a walk. Book and shoe peddlers would come by, and some girls would examine their products, but most gave them a dismissive wave. At ten o'clock, Mrs. Jane would tell us it was time for bed, and I would snuggle into my hollow next to Sally. I could smell her scent, delicate as roses.

Curious about my predecessor, I asked Sally about her. "What was she like? Why did she leave? "

"Annabel was about nineteen and from a farm."

"Just like me?" I squealed. "What color was her hair?"

"Quiet," said Rachel who was in the next bed.

"I'm trying to sleep," said Mary.

"Brown," Sally whispered.

"She had brown hair just like me. I'm sleeping in my twin's place," I laughed quietly.

Sally said, "I hope not."

"Why?" I asked.

Sally's voice sounded different. "If you think that she's your twin, you won't want to hear this."

"Yes, I do." I wasn't scared by anything.

"Well, she got sick, and she went back to her parents."

"And what?"

"And she died," she snapped.

I wondered what she died from. The mill girls didn't stay for a long time. Several had been there for almost four years, but most of them seemed to stay about two years and then move on. Some got married; some went west; others went on to another job.

My bedmate Sally was twenty years old, blond and blue-eyed. Small waisted, she looked delicate, but she had been a weaver for almost a year. She had thought about going into domestic service because she would have better food, more comfortable lodging, and a better salary, but she decided that she didn't want that. She said, "I won't be a slave to someone else's needs." She made me laugh. She was always poking fun at Mrs. Jane. She'd say, "Now, you listen here, you need to go to church and pray hard." We would giggle like little children.

In the close quarters of the boarding house, she helped me adapt to this new life. She was my sister, my best friend. The only problem was that she coughed a lot, which kept me awake. I would burrow into Annabel's hollow and put my hands over my ears so I couldn't hear her, but still the bed shook. One night, I woke from a fretful sleep. Although I was sweaty, I felt cold and vulnerable. Sally was whispering softly, making unrecognizable sounds. I gently pulled her close, feeling the steel rigidity in her small thin body. "It's okay, Sally. I'm here," I whispered.

Sally struggled for breath. "She—She was here. She looked so sad."

"Who are you talking about?"

"Annabel. People see her sometimes." Then she burst into sobs, but she wouldn't tell me why. The other girls stirred in their sleep. Mary snored.

The boarding house meant that I had immediate friends, although the old timers mocked the way I spoke—they said I twanged!—and they laughed at my country clothes. They taught me the city way of speaking and dressing. As soon as I had enough money, I replaced my shawl with a bonnet. The stages and drovers passing daily over the turnpikes brought all sorts of people through town. Coming back from lunch, we would wave at them as they passed. The young men would tip their hats to us, and we would laugh. Life was so much better here than on the farm.

We were like a small village of thirty-six women, who were treated like small children. Mrs. Jane was our surrogate mother. If she had any problems with us, she just went to the mill owner. We would play the piano in the parlors, sing songs like "Barbara Allen, "Lord Lovell," or hymns that we had learned from our parents or at church. I had brought my copy of *The Arabian Nights* with me; Sally had *The Mysteries of Udolpho*; and one of our roommates, Mary, brought *Aesops's Fables* and *Plutarch's Lives.* We received several newspapers and *The Factory Girl's Garland,* which gave us advice about how to handle the men around us. We organized a Self Improvement Circle, where we shared pieces we had written and discussed literature. We were a sisterhood, we told ourselves, feeling very grown up.

On Sundays, we wore our finery to church. We would listen to the sermon, but of course, we were looking to see who else was there. At night, Sally and I would climb into bed and share our dreams of the future. I wanted to earn something of my own so I could have a dowry. She wanted to help her brother get through school, get married, and have four children. She even had their names picked out.

"But then you will go away and leave me," I would grimly point out.

"We'll always be friends."

"I hope so." Her friendship was very important to me. She was my first real friend. You don't make many friends living on a farm surrounded by acres and acres of corn and pumpkins.

She continued. "Besides, you can come visit. Once I'm married, I will have my own home."

I giggled. "Then you will be a Sedate Matron."

"Maybe. But first I have to make the right choice. I cannot give my hand if I can't give my heart first."

"Oh, I agree. Marriage without love would be terrible."

Marriage meant that we had to take a leap of faith. We had to go from our familiar home into a future that we knew little about. It could mean our future happiness or abysmal suffering. We hugged each other good night and went to sleep. She woke up coughing that night. Our roommate Mary told me to put a pillow under her head—that would help stop the coughing.

One weekend her brother Caleb came to Concord and took the two of us out to supper. We ate turkey, lots of vegetables, and Indian pudding. We wore our best bonnets. Sally said she hoped that maybe Caleb and I would like each other; we could marry; and then Sally and I could be sisters AND best friends. But it wasn't to be.

Bells regulated our life. We knew when the bell rang at dawn that it was time to get to work. The sun wasn't even up, and the streets were filled with workers walking to the mill. The bells rang when work started, rang to begin and end meals, and rang to signal the end of the day. We had thirty minutes for breakfast and for our dinner, which was served at noon. We would rush home at noon, wolf down Mrs. Jane's calorie-filled dinner, and race back to work. When the bells tolled at close, we would shut down our machines, descend the lint-covered staircase, and cross the mill yard in the evening light—with our heads aching and ears ringing from all the noise. We worked every day except Sunday. The workday was longest in summer when we stayed at our machines for fourteen hours, with brief breaks for breakfast and dinner. The windows remained shut; it was hard to breathe.

Some workers were barely ten years old. Because they had small hands, they were used to oil machines, remove the full bobbins from the spinning frames, and remove loose threads from inside moving machines. They had to work almost fourteen hours a day. There were some middle-aged women, but most of us were between the ages of seventeen and twenty-four. There were about 100 workers, evenly divided between men and women and native-born Yankees and Irish imigrants. Each stuffy room usually had eighty women at the machines, with two men managing the operation. Although the rooms were hot in the summer and cold in the winter, windows were nailed shut so that the conditions remained optimal for the thread. Of course, that meant particles of thread and cloth filled the air—as if we were in a snowstorm. Some women used snuff to limit the amount of lint they inhaled, but Sally and I thought that was worse than the lint. We stood all day at our machines in the hot, damp, noisy workrooms. One girl fainted three times in one day. She lost her job.

Accidents were commonplace. People got mangled and maimed. One man had his arm caught by the belt. It was amputated at the shoulder. The owner gave him $75 because he would never be able to work again. He was crying when he left. How was he going to live with one arm? One ten-year-old girl let her long hair get too close to the moving machine. It ripped her scalp off her head. That was an awful day. At night, Sally and I would curl up in bed and talk quietly about what we would do when we had enough money saved. She was saving money so her brother could go to school. Every two months, she sent $6 home. I wasn't that organized. I had sent my mother $5 so she could get some material for a new dress for herself and my father $10 so he could get a new plow. I had $20 in my dowry savings account, and one strapping baler whom I had met at church looking my direction.

Now that I felt the jingle of money in my pocket, I knew life was good. I had a best friend, a community of women, a savings account, and a new bonnet. When the weather was good on Sundays, we would walk along the Assabet river that fed the mill. It was a pretty walk, but I got out of breath easily.

On some Saturday nights, we would go into town and see a minstrel show with Mary, Rachel, and the other girls in our room. The center of each minstrel show was the typical minstrel clown with his blackened face, his wooly hair, his thick white lips, his ear-to-ear grin and the banjo on his knees. Around him, a show consisting of music, dance, and comedy was arranged and formed an entertainment program for the white audience. One night, Sally started coughing so badly that people were turning and staring. I pled fatigue so we could leave. That night, after we went to sleep, she began making soft, indecipherable noises and then she began tossing and turning. I woke her up. "Sally. It's okay. It's okay."

When she woke up, she began to sob. "I'm so scared. I saw Annabel again. She looked so sad." I hugged her tightly, feeing the heat of my body seep into her cold damp flesh.

That morning, I noticed some blood drops on Sally's pillowcase. When she saw me staring at it, she turned the pillow over, angrily. "Don't say anything!"

"I won't."

"You better not," she whispered. "It will go away. I know it."

Several weeks later, Mrs. Jane came to Sally and me. "There have been complaints from girls down the hall about your coughing. It's keeping them up."

Sally didn't say anything. So I spoke for the both of us. "I'm sorry."

Some Saturday nights we stayed in and played charades. We would laugh so hard at our silliness that sometimes I couldn't catch my breath. Then of course, the next day we had to go to church and listen to all those prayers. I met a young man there who worked in a factory down the street. He was nice, but he wanted to stay in town.

Sally and I talked about going West. We had heard other girls planning to join an emigration society that was taking people to the West to clear the forests and raise crops. One peddler told us that the corn was as high as an "elephant's eye" and turnips were "five feet tall." We thought it would be a great adventure, but the blood spatters on Sally's pillow were getting worse. And she dreamed more frequently about Annabel.

The mill owner kept close tabs on us. If there was a problem at the boarding house, Mrs. Jane called him and he would decide what to do. One day, one girl accused another of stealing. He listened to each one and then fired them both. He sponsored a school, but when one of the children acted up in school, he threatened not to hire him. He dealt with rowdiness, brawls, and drunks. He was like our father. One morning, he called Sally in and told her that she was keeping the others awake with her coughing—that he was letting her go. She cried, but he didn't change his mind.

When she told me, I cried and cried. I was losing my friend. We said our goodbyes, hugged, and she returned home promising to write. Later that night I dreamed Annabel came to my bed. She sat down besides me and stroked my hair. I could see right through her. Her hair was brown—just like mine—but her face was so sad. I wondered why. When I turned away, I heard her coughing. When I woke up, Mary was putting a pillow under my head, and I realized that I was the one who was coughing. Three weeks later, Sally's brother wrote to me saying that Sally died, but I wasn't surprised. Now I was finding blood on my pillow too, and Annabel came every night.

Historic Damon Mill

The West Concord area where the Damon Mill stands has been associated with industry and manufacturing for several centuries. In the mid-seventeenth century, it was home to iron works, as well as saw, grist, and fulling mills with the Assabet River supplying the necessary power. In the nineteenth century, Concord's industries included the nation's first commercially-produced pencils by William Munroe, the manufacture of lead pipe and sheet lead by David Loring in 1819, Harvey Wheeler's Boston Harness Company 1890, and George Conant Bluine Manufacturing Company for a product to whiten laundry. A wooden mill building more than one hundred feet long where cotton yarn was produced preceded the present building. Calvin Carver Damon purchased the mill in 1834. By the end of the nineteenth century, Damon Mill produced cotton, satinet, and finally domett cloth, a combination of wool and cotton that he invented and successfully marketed.

Today the handsome brick building contains offices but it also contains the ghosts of several young mill girls who left their family farms for a great adventure.

On a Clear Day

Before my mother died in 1781, she would sit me on her lap, saying, "This is my little girl who I was so afraid the Red Coats would get." I would always reassure her, telling her that they didn't get me—that I was safe with her, my brother William, and baby sister Sarah. But she would turn her head to the side and cry and cry.

My brother William, who is three years older than I am, told me that he could remember that day when we ran out the door leaving lame John behind to take care of our home, Munroe Tavern.

But I am getting ahead of myself. Let me start from the beginning.

My father is the great-grandson of the first Munroe, William Munroe, who came to Lexington. Cromwell's soldiers had taken William prisoner at the Battle of Worcester, England, and sent him to the colonies in indentured servitude. He settled in Lexington about 1660, where he began to find a road to success in this new country.

Born in 1742, my father, yet-another William Munroe, married Anna Smith in 1768. They must have had some money because her wedding bonnet came from Paris. I still have her bonnet, parasol, and one of her tiny wedding slippers. Her wedding ring was engraved with "Hearts United Live Contented." And the wedding presents were beautiful pieces of furniture, such as the Sheraton butler's desk with brasses, the Queen Anne tilt-top tea table, and the mahogany Chippendale chest, which are still in the Munroe Tavern. My parents certainly weren't poor Yankees.

Those days, Massachusetts Avenue as we call it now, was a busy dusty road. Many New Hampshire and Vermont drovers took that route going to the Brighton meat markets with their herds of cattle and sheep, and the farmers with their wool, dairy products, and general farm produce used it to head for the Boston markets. My father saw a good business opportunity and purchased "a mansion house, barn, wood house, three-quarters of a potash house with works belonging to it, the 'country store,' and twenty-six acres of land." Built in the early 1690s, the tavern was named for my father, who served as proprietor from 1770 to 1827. At age twenty-eight, he began running the tavern, along with his cooper trade and apple business, and he ran it until his death in 1827—at age eighty-five.

A community center, the tavern was a meeting point for the settlers, who would smack their lips over a Sheffield mug of flip or a glass of hard cider and talk about the latest news from Boston. Some would use the clay pipe free of charge, but they would fill it with the best Virginia tobacco Father could find to sell. Often the drovers would spend the evenings in the taproom and the nights in the barns.

The Munroe Tavern at 1322 Massachusetts Avenue is located one mile east of Lexington Common. Like the Hancock-Clarke House, Munroe Tavern and Buckman Tavern are properties of the Lexington Historical Society and open to the public. *Courtesy of Paul E. Doherty*

The tavern had a taproom, a large kitchen, rooms upstairs for guests and family, and small fireplaces, which burned peat instead of wood. It also had stables, which could hold one hundred horses. In 1770, the year before I was born, my father added the 30- x 60-foot ell for dancing and parties. He even had a fiddler's throne, which is a raised portion of the floor for a band to sit on when playing.

Rules of the Tavern

Four pence a night for bed
Six pence with supper
No more than five to sleep in one bed
No boots to be worn in bed
Organ grinders to sleep in the wash-house
No dogs allowed in the kitchen
No razor grinders or tinkers taken in

Like many of the village residents, my father was also a soldier. He was the Orderly Sergeant of the Lexington militia on April 18, 1775. On the night when he heard that the British were coming, he told Mother that he had to go to the Hancock-Clarke House where John Hancock and Samuel Adams were staying.

He called John Raymond in from his room in the barn. Once the owner of the tavern just down the road, John now worked for us. Mother always shook her head about John. "Poor John," she would say, "Here, he has a bad leg, and he ended up bearing his family's financial problems. And he has all those children!"

Father would reply, "But aren't we lucky to have him helping us?" John helped bring in the wood and took care of horses when need be.

Mother added. "And his family has a roof over its head, thanks to Lydia Mulliken purchasing his tavern."

We all liked John. He was always carving us things: He made William a top a small wooden doll for me, which I called Jane. My rag doll was easier to play with, but Jane was the one I could talk to. I told her all my secrets.

Father told him, "Now, John, I have to go to town and protect John Hancock and Sam Adams. I want you to protect my family."

"Of course. I will be proud to." John patted my head and winked at William. "William and I will be sure that everyone is safe." William drew himself up proudly.

"Good." Father left. Mother looked shaky but continued to mix her bread in a wooden trough and set it to rise. Then she put us to bed.

Supposedly, Father was there at the parsonage when Revere galloped up. Later he told us that he had said to Revere, "The family has just retired and requested that they not be disturbed by noise."

Revere snapped at him. "Noise! You will have noise enough before long, The Regulars are coming out."

Early the next morning, father led John Hancock, Sam Adams, Paul Revere, and John Lovell, Hancock's secretary, to north Lexington, where he hid them. Then he returned and joined his compatriots and Captain Parker on the Common, where the belfry bell was sounding the alarm.

That morning, we could hear the tramp tramp of marching soldiers and the clip clop of horses going down Lexington Road. When we looked out, we saw the scarlet uniforms of the British through the morning fog. Their bayonets gleaming, the British regulars marched down the road with practiced precision. In several minutes, we heard beating drums and pealing bells. John came out of the barn, shouting, "Mrs. Munroe, Mrs. Munroe. This looks bad. Don't you go outside now."

My mother frowned and bit her lip. "Stay inside, children." We heard nothing, until the gunfire. There was a lot of it, followed by silence and then shouting.

Built about 1698, the Hancock-Clarke House at 36 Hancock Street, Lexington, was the home of the Reverend John Hancock, grandfather of John Hancock, the first signer of the Declaration of Independence and the first Governor of Massachusetts. His successor, Reverend Jonas Clarke, an ardent supporter for American independence, was known for his passionate sermons. The night of April 18, 1775, John Hancock and Samuel Adams, prominent patriots, were visiting Reverend Clarke in the parsonage. John Hancock's aunt and his fiancée, Dorothy Quincy, were also staying in the house. That night, Boston's Dr. Joseph Warren sent William Dawes and Paul Revere to Lexington with news of the advancing British troops. Arriving separately, they stopped to warn Hancock and Adams and then set off for Concord. Today, this evening is reenacted the night before Patriot's Day. The Hancock-Clarke house is of particular interest because it contains furnishings and portraits owned by the Hancock and Clarke families and treasured relics of April 19. Today, it is the property of the Lexington Historical Society. *Courtesy of Paul E. Doherty*

My mother grabbed up the family silver, telling us, "Come with me, children." She dug a hole under the big oak standing on the hill behind the tavern, placed the silver in it and then mounded the dirt back over it. I picked the violets that were just beginning to bloom. William ran around with a stick, pretending it was a gun and that he was killing the British, and baby Sarah crawled in the grass. But then it was time for chores. I fed the chickens while William milked the cows. When we were done, William wanted to walk into town to see what had happened, Mother looked hesitant.

John Raymond, who had appeared at that moment, said, "Ma'm, I'd recommend that you all stay here. We don't know what's happening uptown, but it's probably nothing very good since Mr. Munroe isn't back."

She smiled grimly. "You're absolutely right, John. Children, we will stay here and turn over the garden. Soon we will be planting."

William started to say something. Mother snapped, "No, I tell you, William. Now you go help John Raymond take the animals to the meadow to graze and then clean the pens. And Anna, you watch over your sister, while I take care of the wash. Then we will get the garden ready for planting."

The day was a perfect April day: low clouds racing through the sky, flickering sun light through the soft chartreuse buds of the trees. We almost forgot that Father had gone off with his musket and that soldiers had marched down the road. Later that afternoon, we heard the tromp tromp of feet again. John, who had been telling us a story about his children, got up from where he was sitting, saying he was going to see what was happening. He came back as fast as a man with a lame foot could, saying, "A British officer with hundreds of men and two cannon is marching down the road towards us."

Suddenly, we heard the booming of cannon and smelled smoke. Mother ran around, grabbing food and clothes, telling me, "Get your sister, now." I began crying for my doll, and she snapped, "If you want to take your doll, you need to get it. Now!" Baby Sarah was crying, and William was saying that he was going to stay with John to protect the tavern.

"No you're not," said Mother. "You're coming with me. To protect us."

"I can't find my doll," I cried. "I need to find her."

John Raymond stooped down and hugged me. "I will find your dolly and keep it safe for you."

"You promise?" I sniffled.

"Of course. I made her for you after all." William looked at John, and he nodded. "You go with your Mother, sonny." John hugged me again. "You be a big girl now. Help your mother to take care of Sarah."

By the time the British soldiers approached the tavern, we were running out the back door. My mother held me by my hand, Sarah in her arms, and William ran by her side. As she ran from the house, one of the soldiers started to fire, but an officer knocked his arm and said, "British soldiers do not fire on a woman." As she told the story later, we could hear the cannon firing over our heads on the hill. We could smell the smoke of the three buildings, which the British burned between here and the center of Lexington. And we still did not know what was happening to Father who left early that morning.

That afternoon of April 19, 1775, the Munroe Tavern served as the headquarters for Brigadier General Earl Percy and his one thousand reinforcements. The British commandeered the tavern for one and one-half hours. The Regulars coming back from Concord dropped exhausted on the grass; the taproom was converted into a field hospital; and John Raymond tried to keep up with their unruly demands for food and drink. When they began to leave, one Regular, who probably had too much to drink, shot at the ceiling, leaving a souvenir that is still there. The Regulars piled up our furniture and set it afire.

Later that afternoon, when my father returned from the battle and we returned from hiding, my parents wouldn't let us go into the tavern. They made us stay outside, but while they were agonizing over the blood and old bandages on the taproom floor and half-burned household furniture, I found John Raymond, lying on his stomach just outside the back doorway. A bullet had gone through his back. In his hand he held my wooden doll. Forty-four years old, he left his wife and five children: John Jr., Eliakim, Rebecca, Isaac, and Edmund.

Munroe Inn keepers have reported signs of ghosts in the inn. One account was quite specific. The first night the caretaker locked one outside and two internal sets of doors before climbing into bed. She was awakened by creaking noises and the sound of door latches opening and shutting. The next day, she found that the outside door was still locked, but the two inside doors were opened and unlocked. By the fourth day, she was turning on the radio at night to block out the obstreperous ghosts. Sometimes she thought that someone was in the bedroom; she heard footsteps going up the stairs. Certainly, that ghost must be John Raymond seeking to protect the Inn and its belongings—even if it is only a little girl's doll.

Historic Munroe Tavern

The Munroe Tavern, at 1332 Massachusetts Avenue, is located one mile east of Lexington Common. The bullet hole in the ceiling and many family articles from this period are on display in the tavern, including an eighteenth-century tavern sign. President Washington dined at the Munroe Tavern when he visited the Lexington battlefield in 1789; an upstairs room contains the table at which he sat, documents relating to his trip, and a fine wooden tricorn hatbox dating from the Revolutionary period. Munroe Tavern is open weekends from April—June and daily in the summer.

Lydia Mulliken purchased the Raymond house/tavern in 1774, and permitted the Raymond family to live there at least until April 19, 1775. In 1795 Lydia's son John tore down the tavern and built the house that stands on the site of 1377 Massachusetts Avenue today.

A Very Lovely Club

B y the mid nineteenth century, new ideas about nationalism, expansion, and slavery were sweeping the country. The railroads to urban centers such as Boston and New York were changing how people lived and worked. As the twentieth century approached, my parents and their friends were talking about the advantages of family life in a country setting where the air and water were pristine. Father, like many others, was part of the huge middle class, which grew out of the Industrial Revolution. Although he wasn't exactly the captain of industry—much less a robber baron, he wanted to own a turreted, towered, multi-chimneyed home on a large green-grass square. Now that the railroad was part of American life, Father could travel to his well-paying job in the city, while raising his family in the clean country air far away from the city's harmful influence. So like many Bostonians who found their calling in railroads, textiles, or banking, we moved to the suburbs—to Lexington, Massachusetts.

Until this time, Lexington residents were primarily Yankee farmers and tradesmen, some of whom were descendents of those who had stood on the Lexington Common that fateful April morning in 1775. During the second half of the nineteenth century, many Irish had moved into this Protestant setting to be confronted by age-old prejudice and signs saying, "Irish need not apply." When they found jobs, the men worked as laborers for the railroad or on the farms, and the women worked as household help. Many of them lived across the railroad tracks in an area known as 'Skunk Hollow' on the streets now called Woburn, Vine, and Cottage. People like my parents and their friends, who were often temperance advocates, viewed them as poorly educated, quarrelsome whiskey drinkers. Needless to say, my parents did not mingle with the Irish, heaven forbid, and I was supposed to ignore them.

My parents and their friends did not see that they had much in common with Lexington's farmers, merchants, and tradesmen. They were the new power structure; the latter were the people who maintained that system. When my parents left Boston for the pastoral charms of a town that held a significant place in history, they moved into a town in the midst of transition. It had plenty of bucolic charm, but those picturesque cows grazing on the meadows did leave manure on the muddy roads. It didn't have much crime, but it didn't have much plumbing either. Although the middle class wanted the rural charm of the suburbs, they also wanted the urban amenities. These new residents made sure that the utilities, streets, and sewers were improved, the police force increased, and moral reforms such as temperance fostered. They extolled the charms of living in the suburbs and developed Meriam and Munroe Hills. More businessmen moved to Lexington and began to sit on town boards and committees, becoming a major force in town affairs.

Many prominent Lexingtonians belonged to Hancock Congregational or First Parish Unitarian Universalist Church, but they needed more than Sunday services to satisfy the social desires of their wives. The latter didn't want just the church socials but crested and engraved, invitation-only cotillions. They held "at home" parties in the winter, lawn parties in the summer, and tea parties in the afternoon. When the snow was right, they even illuminated the toboggan slide on Oakland Street for their enjoyment. Now, I really liked that!

In 1892, Lexington's most influential residents built an exclusive club to encourage temperance, social exchange, and athletic pursuits. They raised almost $14,000 for the clubhouse and charged the limited membership an annual fee of $15 in a time when the average laborer and domestic servant made $350-$400 annually. Certainly, the Irish wouldn't be joining. This exclusive club, known as the Old Belfry Club or the OBC, played a major role in the life of Lexington's upper classes— much to my mother's delight. Situated at the intersection of Muzzey and Forest Streets, the club was most handsome according to Mother's friends. They marveled at the ornate wallpapers and richly colored paints that covered the walls and coveted the oriental rugs and bearskins that covered the floors. The club had a library and a ladies' reading room.

I always found that term, "ladies" reading room, interesting. Who was a lady and who wasn't? What would happen if a non-lady entered that room? Would they throw her out or would they turn their backs to her and freeze her out? Ladies, my Mother told me, were white people, who went to the Protestant churches, and who wore gloves and hats when going into the city. "Thus far," she informed me, "You have failed to meet my standards for a lady." She had caught me climbing a tree; I picked my neighbor's flowers without permission; and I went wading in a pond with the boy down the road. In summation, she said, "I despair of you ever becoming a lady Eliza Sue. You will be the death of me yet."

I said, "Yes ma'm. I'm sorry, Ma'm." I endeavored to look very sorrowful, although I wasn't sorrowful—by any means. I thought being a lady was totally boring!

The club members took their leisure very seriously. They came to play tennis, billiards, and croquet; to dance, to dine, and to flirt. They came to compete, to impress, and to enjoy this life of entertainment. And it was fun. The OBC had bowling alleys in the basement, a billiard room, and tennis courts adjacent to the porch. Its members enjoyed weekly tennis tournaments, often followed by afternoon tea. In 1922, the OBC season (mid-October to April) included eleven formal dances with orchestras, three concerts, two lectures, a members' frolic and a members' gambol. Children were offered different activities, while teenagers attended dances and subscription parties, which included music and dancing—well chaperoned, of course. The OBC offered plays, carnivals, and fun nights. There were bridge and whist nights. Sometimes it even held lectures on global issues. Helen Keller came to talk once.

Upstairs, there was an enormous ballroom with a stage. The ballroom not only held all the dancers, but all the people who were there to watch and gossip. The Fox Trot, which was a fast trotting step to a new jazz beat called "ragtime," was just becoming popular when I started going to OBC. Later, the Charleston and Swing became popular. The older ladies had a lot to say about the way the new knee-length dresses embroidered with glass beads and paillettes would swing rhythmically according to the dancers' movements. The young women sometimes wore powder, rouge, and pale blue eye shadow, and the older women whispered that one or two even plucked their eyebrows!

It was a lovely club for desirable people with a definite code of behavior. No alcohol, gambling, or petitions. No immigrants with any peculiar habits and dangerous religious practices. No one was allowed to speak meanly to staff members. Its membership was limited, which meant that it was for the social elite.

Mother and her friends looked like Gibson Girls, with their hourglass, tiny-waisted figures. They wore corsets and piled their hair high on their heads. Luckily, I was still young enough at age thirteen that I didn't have to wear a corset, but I did have to wear a sailor collar. When it was cold, I had to wear a long vest with suspenders to keep up my scratchy woolen stockings. Father wore a cutaway frock coat, with a bowler hat and carried a silver cane.

The other OBC members looked just like my parents. They dressed the same, shopped in the same stores, and went to the same Protestant churches. Their manners were perfect, and they regulated emotional displays as stringently as they did their bodies. Extremes of sadness or happiness were to be avoided along with heavy or abstract topics. They all had the same chalky white skin—like the underbelly of a fish I thought—and pinched little mouths surrounding straight white teeth. They smelled of rose-scented talcum powder or, if they were older, lavender.

Mother and her friends signed us up for dancing classes. I didn't like any of the other children who went to the OBC. One or two were in my class at school, but we weren't friends. At dancing school, we all had to wear white gloves, and the girls had to wait for the boys to bow in front of them, requesting a dance. There we sat on a row of chairs, waiting for the dancing teacher to click her clicker, and then a herd of boys would come over to our side. Of course, I didn't want to be picked, but if no one asked me to dance —well, I would be a wallflower! Talk about the kiss of death! The boy who always asked me to dance was named Aloysius; he smelled of Vicks Vapor Rub. I despised him.

Mother talked a lot about civility, refinement, and gentility; she said I was missing those qualities that a lady needed. I said I didn't really want to be a lady—that it struck me as rather dull—that all this talk about deportment was boring. She sent me to my room. Mother said I was a reckless tomboy. That I would get freckles if I didn't watch out—and no lady ever had freckles. I didn't think I was reckless; I just liked being outside rather than sitting on a chair with my feet neatly tucked beneath me. I wanted to dive into the pond, climb the tree, and swing on the rope over the brook. I didn't want to sit and sew, write in my diary, or practice piano. I was told to never scratch my head, pick my teeth, clean my nails, or worse of all, pick my nose in company.

When I went to father, he said a lady was a woman who made a man act like a gentleman. When I looked confused, he laughed. Then he told me to talk to mother.

My Irish friends at school referred to the OBC members as "highfaluting," and then they would sniff and toss their heads. I didn't want to tell them that my parents were members and that I too had appeared at an OBC function in my dreaded sailor collar. They would never let me live that down.

Father said when I complained, "If you wish to be a refined American girl, you do the things your mother taught you."

Mother sighed and said, "The OBC provides a place to meet people like us."

"What does that mean?" I asked.

She paused, "Well, it's a place to meet desirable people—well-bred people who have a sense of propriety, who are in the better social circles."

"I don't understand."

She sniffed, "Well, there are some people that you don't need to know." I disagreed of course. I found friendships in my classmates, the O'Haras, MacDonalds, and the Caseys. They were great fun, even though some of them sported unladylike freckles. I just didn't tell my parents about them.

"Like who?" I asked, but she didn't tell me, which didn't matter, for I knew who she was referring to. She was speaking of the Irish, whom she characterized as loud talking, laughing, and poorly mannered!

I went to Hancock School, and one of my best friends was Mary O'Hara, whose father was a live-in groundskeeper on Meriam Hill. Mary still talked about her first communion at St. Bridget's, which sounded much more exciting than being confirmed. She was given a party and a fancy white dress; when she was older, she would be able to pick a new name. I would pick Eve if I could. Mary told me stories about wee folk, leprechauns, and banshees warning of oncoming death. She had three older brothers who teased her about her red hair and freckles, but they looked out for her. At parties at her house, teary-eyed people sang of the River Shannon and the green hills of Donegal. And yes, they drank whiskey.

Mother didn't know that I had ever visited Mary's house with its outdoor plumbing. She always suggested that I play with Vanessa White, who was a stuffy little prig. So I kept Mary as my secret.

One day I heard Mother and her friend talking in the front parlor. "Isn't the OBC just wonderful—how it helps us get away from it all."

"I agree, my dear," said my Mother. "People with common interests…"

"I really don't see the need to mix with certain people—you know who I mean!"

"Of course."

"You don't allow Eliza Sue to play with those children, do you?"

"Well, I certainly don't let her go to their houses, but she does go to Lexington's schools, and they do mingle there."

"And what do you think about that? There they are with their beer, their saints, having a child every year, and …"

"Enough," Mother snapped. "That comment isn't worthy of you, my dear."

I have to say this for my Mother: She was a snob, but she wasn't as bad as her friend.

The OBC is long gone, or at least we can't see it anymore, but occasionally—on those moonless nights—we can see those ghosts, frock-coated and tiny-waisted, from the past and hear those same beliefs expressed.

The Curmudgeon

"Do you know that the average gray squirrel can leap immense voids, climb colossal buildings, hang from thin wires, and lunge onto bird feeders from lofty branches?" Joe yelled from the other side of the hedge.

Audrey shook her head. He was obviously on a squirrel-hating binge again. It happened every winter. A long-time widower, Joe had become more irascible the older he got and the more bourbon he drank. He was her neighbor, however, and she too was alone. They got along. Sometimes she had him to supper, and he would tell her about the different birds in the area. She liked that. At one point, she even found herself wondering if they should be closer—become better friends. She had thought about asking him to come to church with her, but he was quite cantankerous and sometimes he smelled rather ripe. So she left the relationship as it was: an occasional drink, a conversation over the fence, a ride when her car was in the shop…

"Now, Joe," she said, stepping around the end of the hedge.

"Don't now me, young lady." He growled. "The *Sciurus carolinensis*—that's the fancy Latin term for those rodents—can jump three to four feet straight up and can leap horizontally around ten to twelve feet. And they can run—their average speed, at a full run, is between eight and ten mph. "

"That's fast," Audrey gasped. "Imagine a squirrel coming at you that quickly!"

"I refuse to let that bushy-tailed rat defeat me. He's keeping all the cardinals away from my feeders."

"At Garden Club, Mabel talked about greasing or oiling the bird feeler post so the squirrels would just slide down."

"Those blasted rodents are persistent problem solvers. They look at any thing you do as a challenge. To outmaneuver a squirrel, you need to consider its behavior." He spat in disgust. I winced. He continued, "If you hang a feeder from a tree, you are on the squirrel's turf—and in trouble."

"What about reversing your strategy? You could feed them? You know those corn cobs they sell?"

"You're suggesting that I feed the little devils?" He guffawed. Sparrows, blue jays, and even a cardinal flew by; a mourning dove was waddling under his feeder.

"Well, yes I guess I am, but you are already, aren't you?"

"What are you implying?"

"I'm talking about all that thistle seed, corn, and sunflower seed they're eating out of your feeders." A house finch hopped on to the feeder.

He snorted, "They're not supposed to be eating that. It's for the birds. Don't you understand? I want to get rid of the squirrels—not encourage more of them. If I were younger, I'd rig up a slingshot or get a BB gun."

Audrey shivered. She was getting cold just standing there. "Oh Joe, you can't kill them. That's against the law. The animal control officer would come after you."

"Fat chance. Maybe I'll give them the swim test." His eyes glittered.

"You're just trying to rile me, Joe. Lexington's a no-hate town, remember."

"Not when it comes to me and squirrels, young lady; Squirrels carry the SAME diseases (plus a few) as rats, and they are not afraid of people. I'll show them." He stomped off.

Well, Audrey thought, she did like being called a young lady at age fifty-five. But Joe's temper was a bit much at times. She finished raking her leaves. They needed to be up before the first snow fall. She looked up at the big locust tree in Joe's yard. High up in its branches was a squirrel's drey, a collection of sticks and leaves they called a nest. The cardinal sang from the old apple tree, as she piled the leaves in her plastic leaf bag. She shivered. Winter was coming quickly to Lexington this year.

That night, Joe went to bed dreaming about how to conquer the squirrels. He could try to evict them. He could use peanut butter as bait and trap them. Then he would have the problem of what to do with the varmints. He knew some who had given them the swim test, but these days, in a town that was as environmentally friendly as Lexington, his neighbors would not approve. How could he possibly hurt a cute little squirrel?

Easily, he thought. But if he released the squirrel miles from his home, he might find some new enemies in his life. No one else wanted the beast. And what if he got stopped, and people saw that he had a squirrel in the trap in his car. He'd have to kill them, he thought. And soon before they took over.

Something woke him up in the early gray chill before dawn—he thought he heard someone whispering, but no one could be in the house. He lay there, listening until he realized it wasn't whispering but a gentle scuttling noise overhead. The squirrels had moved in. They were taking over, dammit! They had become invaders. The cold weather had driven them to his warm attic, where they would find all sorts of things to chew. He sighed. He could hear the squirrels moving, shifting, whispering up there. Sometimes he heard long shrill sounds. They were even calling to each other, he thought, probably telling all their friends to move in.

The next day it snowed. It was an early December snowstorm, and traffic was a mess. The governor suggested that businesses close down, if possible, and let their employees go early, but everyone left at once so the roads were a mess. People were caught in massive traffic jams and running out of gas as the snow piled up. Joe stayed in the house listening to the squirrels scampering back and forth. By noon, there was a new noise coming from above—like chewing on pipes. An evil brown syrupy stain began to discolor his bedroom ceiling. He opened another bottle of Jim Beam, picked up the broom, and hammered on the ceiling. "That will scare them," he thought. "Damn rodents!"

All he could hear now was the howl of the north wind and the crunch of snow and ice against the windows. He poured himself a stiff bourbon, congratulating himself, and went to bed, leaving the broom nearby.

It was four in the morning, when he heard the scuttling sound again. One noise was coming from directly overhead, another from the far corner. *Damn those varmints,* he thought and put the pillow over his head. But he could hear them still. This wasn't a dream. He sat up, got out of bed, grabbed his broom, and pounded on the ceiling again. The stain was now the size of a dinner plate. The scuttling stopped, and then it began again. It was

Squirrels can be more than a nuisance.
Courtesy of D. Peter Lund

even louder than before. He sat up. "I'm seventy years old, dammit. I don't need this. They're laughing at me up there. I'm going to gas them, tomorrow." He sat back down on the bed.

Suddenly, he heard a new noise—closer by. He looked up. A squirrel was entering his bedroom. At the door squatted another, its tail jerking spasmodically. The first one stopped in front of him and sat back on its haunches. "Well, look at you, you little rat," said Joe, reaching for his broom. The squirrel made a long shrill *tchhh* sound. Joe shouted back at it. The squirrel jumped at him—just below his chin—its teeth pierced his throat, where it tore the skin to shreds in an instant. Joe started to get out of his chair, and then two squirrels jumped at him.

They're only little things, he thought. *I can brush them off.* One jumped on his shoulder, clawing at his face. The other went for his ear. He could feel a great surging gush splattering down to his shirt. He opened his mouth to scream. Something jumped for his stomach, biting through his pants, and Joe fell to the ground with his scream still trapped inside.

The house was sold after Joe's death, but Audrey often saw a realtor running out of the front door, screaming, "The squirrels are chasing me." Although a new family has moved in, there are many squirrels still around. Can a squirrel actually haunt a house?

Room 24

ike many New England towns, Concord has an appealing cluster of churches, stores, and homes centered around a tidy village green called Monument Square. Convenient to Boston and Cambridge, the charming town offers a small, neat base in a pastoral environment of open fields and lovely woodlands. It also has a ghost.

The rambling Colonial Inn faces one end of Monument Square. Listed on the National Register of Historic Places, the original structure of the inn was built in 1716 by Captain John Minot, a soldier and physician. In 1775, the colonials used one of the buildings as a storehouse for arms and provisions. Dr. Timothy Minot, who owned the building, helped care for the wounded there on April 19, 1775. During the first half of the nineteenth century, parts of the inn were used as a variety store, and parts were used as a residence. From 1835-1837, Henry David Thoreau, his parents, sisters, and brothers lived in the West House with his aunts, Betsy and Sarah. In the latter part of the nineteenth century, the Minot house became part of the inn, along with two nineteenth-century buildings that were added to it.

Guests of the inn have included Franklin D. Roosevelt, J.P. Morgan, John Wayne, Shirley Temple, Steve Martin, Kurt Russell, Goldie Hawn, Arnold Palmer, Faye Dunaway, Dan Quayle, Ritchie Havens, Glenn Close, Bruce Springsteen, Queen Noor of Jordan, and Harry Connick Sr.

In 1966, a newlywed couple, M.P. and Judith Fellenz of Highland Falls, New York, stayed in Room 24, in the 1716 part of the Inn. The bride awoke that night sensing a presence in the room—a feeling that some unknown being was in the midst. She said, "As I opened my eyes, I saw a grayish figure at the side of my bed, to the left, about four feet away. It was not a distinct person, but a shadowy mass in the shape of a standing figure. It remained still for a moment, then slowly floated to

Concord's Colonial Inn at 48 Monument Square, Concord, was originally built in 1716, and has operated as a hotel since 1889. *Courtesy of D. Peter Lund*

the foot of the bed, in front of the fireplace. After pausing a few seconds, the apparition slowly melted away."

She said later that she was so frightened that she could not scream. She also could not sleep.

"For the remainder of the night, I tried to conjure a logical explanation for the apparition. It was not a reflection of the moon as all the curtains were completely closed. Upon relating the incident to my husband, he said the ghost was included in the price of the room."

Obviously, the husband had a great sense of humor, but those who were downstairs that morning remember that the bride looked rather pale. About two weeks later, Loring Grimes, the Innkeeper at that time, received a letter from Mrs. Fellenz. It read in part:

"I have always prided myself on being a fairly sane individual but on the night of June 14, I began to have my doubts. On that night, I saw a ghost in your Inn. The next morning I felt too foolish to mention it to the management, so my husband and I continued on our honeymoon. I wondered whether or not any sightings of a ghost had been reported or if any history of one was involved in the history of the Inn."

More ghostly reports quickly followed. Some just felt the presence of another or saw the outline of a face or figure to the left of the fireplace. Others experienced a prickling sensation and bad dreams. Two ghost hunting teams (Ghost Images Paranormal Investigations and Spirit Encounters Research Team) investigated. One team sensed a good deal of pain and suffering and temperature changes in the room. Some even felt themselves being touched. The manager at the time told them that the original structure was used as a hospital during the Revolutionary War and that Room 24 was Dr. Minot's.

One of these days, more may be known, but at this point, Room 24 is a popular room at the Colonial Inn. If you want to stay there, you need to book it months ahead.

Age of the Silver Screen

Since 1918, I have been the organist for the Lexington Theater. For eight years, I have played the theater's "mighty Wurlitzer" to accompany the silent films. Usually, the studio would send a cue sheet with the film, which I would learn. So most of my time is spent in the darkened theater playing orchestral sounds along with a number of sound effects for such films as *Ben-Hur* or *The Big Parade*. I live in the world of Mary Pickford and Clara Bow. Slim, the blue-collar steel worker, Bull, the Bowery bartender, and Jim, the wealthy son of a mill owner from *The Big Parade,* were my friends. I play the music as the boot camp enlistees, including Slim, Jim, and Bull, did their first full-uniformed march as infantrymen—hundreds of them—marching and singing optimistically as they proceed into France:

> *You're in the army now,*
> *You're not behind a plow;*
> *You'll never get rich,*
> *You son-of-a-gun,*
> *You're in the army now!*

Everytime I see Jim kiss Melisande on her forehead, I weep. A romance is what I need. Sweet romance is something I didn't have. I am thirty-two years old, an old maid, who lives at home with my mother, and who never had a date. I don't know why I am so alone, but I am. When the New Year came, my mother asked me what I wanted. I said to be kissed by a man. She turned red and muttered that kissing wasn't what it was cracked up to be.

So I work in the Lexington Theater, trying to synchronize the music with the film. I eat my cheese sandwich alone at the theater before the matinee, heating my tea in the small kitchen upstairs. At the end of my workday, I walk home alone.

Not much happens in my gray little world. I go to church with my mother, fill in at her bridge table, listen to her friends' chatter, knit sweaters that no one wears, and read romance novels. I still wear my long dark hair loosely on top of my head. I look like women did before the war with my long straight skirt and high collar shirt. The war is long over, but I haven't changed with the times for I have no reason too. A whole generation of young men died in the war, leaving nearly a whole generation of young women like me without possible suitors. Unless I am willing to waste away my life waiting idly for spinsterhood, I have to start enjoying life, but I am not sure how to go about doing that. So I remain stuck here at home with Mother. The one positive thing I have done was to buy a bicycle, which gives me some freedom. On sunny mornings, when I am not working or doing my chores at home, I ride all over Lexington.

Today, an attractive young man came over to me on the organ bench in between shows. We are showing *The Phantom of the Opera* this week.

"Hi," said he, his blue eyes flashing just like they do in the novels. "I'm curious about your work here. Do you enjoy it?"

I feel my heart fluttering. "Oh, yes, I love the films."

"But don't you end up knowing all the subtitles?"

"All the subtitles? Well, yes." I hesitate for a moment, studying him as he shifts his body so to face me more directly. His nose crinkles slightly as if I've asked him a vexing question, and then he smiles. A small gap separates his front teeth. He's just like I pictured some of my romantic heroes. And that makes me bold. This is just like my stories, but it's uncharted territory for me. I laugh up at him just like Clara Bow would do. "I know all the actions, too."

"You do?" He inclines his head toward me and comes closer. "Such as…"

"Pick a movie," I suggest.

"Well, I can't pick *Phantom* because you've watched it all week. You probably can recite all the subtitles."

I laugh, tossing my hair. I'm Mary Pickford now.

"How about *Big Parade*?" he continued. "What happens when Jim opens the food package sent by his girlfriend?"

"Well, there's a hand-written note, which says, "I wish you could be here but the thought that you will soon be leading your men into battle fills me with pride. I suppose the fragrance of beautiful flowers fills the air of your picturesque surroundings. I baked the cake for you myself. Forever, Justyn." And then the cake is absolutely rock hard."

He laughed. "You're good."

This attractive man thinks I'm funny! He sits down next to me on the bench. "I hope you don't mind."

Of course, I don't mind. It's the first time anyone has ever sat on my bench! His eyes are the same color as the morning sky.

"So, the studio sends you the music…"

"Yes. See here." I point at the cue sheet, and begin to play their newest version of the Army song.

We're in the army now,
And we have all learned how
To wash our shirty…"

He began to sing along with the rest of it.

We rub our socks
Till we wear out the rocks,
We're in the army now!…
We drown the fleas
In our Bee Vee Dees,
We're in the army now!"

"You are a good singer," I say.

"Thanks, my mother tells me I am." He stands up. "My name is Marcus, by the way. I already know your name."

"You do?"

"You're Katy, the player of the mighty Lexington Wurlitzer."

I can feel myself blushing. He found out my name before he even came over to talk.

"Well, I have to get going. Thank you for your time."

My heart falls. He has brought more excitement in this brief conversation than I've felt in years.

"I'll probably come and bother you again." He touches my hand very lightly, sending shivers up my arm.

"Oh, that's okay," I say, feeling my face flame. *Okay? Who am I kidding? I'm thrilled!*

That night, I roll around my bed, not sleeping, wondering if he would come back. Closing my eyes, I allow myself to imagine what could come next. His hand would brush my cheek...he would look deep into my eyes...then he would open his mouth...underneath my flannel nightgown, my body stirs. Maybe he's my Prince Charming. I certainly have waited long enough!

He returns; he comes day after day. He sits down on my bench and turns the score for me. When the theater is empty, we talk about the films. He likes them as much as I do. I tell him how the organ brings the show alive. The goal is for the audience to not even recognize that I'm here, even though I'm sitting stage left.

Ever since I met Marcus, I am unable to stop thinking about him. I lie in my narrow childhood bed, dreaming, until Mother calls me for breakfast. He asks me questions about living in town, and I tell him about my quiet life here. One day, he brings me some daisies that he had picked. No one has ever brought me flowers before. Another day, he holds my hand, against the keyboard, and outlines it with his own fingers.

I ride my bicycle all over town, looking for lush green meadows and sparkling ponds. Perhaps we can have a picnic by one of them. I will pack champagne and bonbons—they always sound so romantic—and he will pop them in my mouth as his fingers work at my buttons...

I abandon my more restrictive undergarments and shorten my hems. All Marcus has to do is look at me, and I feel tremors across my nerve endings. When his eyes meet mine, I feel the same tingling sensation in my face.

One day, he reaches into his pocket and pulls out a small porcelain cat. He hands it to me.

"For me?" I ask.

"When I'm not here, I want you to think of me. Put him so you can see him when you play."

Does he think I could ever forget him? My finger strokes the cold smooth porcelain. I am not alone anymore. Someone likes me. I can hardly wait for night to come so I can dream of him and for the next day to come so I can see him again.

I buy a pair of flesh-colored rayon stockings. When I wear them the next day, mother is shocked. She says that real ladies don't expose their skin. That people can see my legs through the stockings and they don't cover me like my old black ones did.

The Gold Rush comes to town. When the Little Tramp is getting ready for New Year's Eve, he sets the table with lighted candles, table napkins, and a heart-shaped place card on his girl's seat, with "To My Love" written on it. Maybe Marcus will take me to dinner, I think. He will look soulfully in my eyes, and he will know how much I loved him, and…

I go to the hairdresser and have her bob my hair. My ears look so naked. Marcus says he loves my ears. He traces his finger around one, which sends little shivers of excitement up and down my spine. Before each matinee, he comes in with that lilt in his step and his eyes twinkling. I can feel my heart pounding in response.

My mother is astounded. "What is happening to you? First, you're showing off your naked legs, and next I know you're cutting your beautiful hair. I suppose now you're going to be wanting to paint your nails? "

I look at my boring hands visualizing them with long red-painted nails. "That might be fun," I say dreamily as I set the table for us. "What are we having for supper, Ma?"

" I can't believe you, Katy. You are not the little girl I brought up to know right from wrong."

I sigh. I have to interrupt her before she got going on this again. "What's for supper?"

"Boiled fowl with egg sauce, mashed turnips, and boiled rice. Don't change the subject. What will the neighbors think? My daughter with naked legs…"

"And for dessert…?"

"Bread and butter pudding."

My life—until I met Marcus—was like Mother's suppers—boring, bland, mind numbing. Now, I feel like I'm glowing—that I can break into that daring new dance, the Charleston, at any moment. I ride my bicycle and let the wind blow through my hair. Marcus seems to fill all the space around me with his pulsing energy. He makes me feel alive in a way that I had never been.

After today's matinee, the manager calls me into his office to speak me about my accompaniment. He says it's rather off key—that I have to do better. Of course, I haven't been thinking about the score but about Marcus who sits by my side in the darkened theater. I'm not worried.

The next afternoon, I see his face, profiled against the view of an endless trail of prospectors in the Klondike of Alaska in 1898. They —along with Charlie Chaplin—were winding their way along to seek their fortunes. I realize that I too am seeking something—a romance. Suddenly, his finger is under my chin, and he turns my face towards him. The pressure of his fingers is lighter than snow falling and a hundred times more intense. He tastes like the movies—exciting and intense. I almost think I can hear the Alaskan winds until I realize it's just the sound of my own heart pounding. While the cabin in *The Gold Rush* teeters back and forth on the edge of the cliff, Marcus' hands go places where no other hands have ever been. And at the final kiss between Charlie Chaplin and Georgia, Marcus kisses me, while I try to play the final melody.

I buy a red cloche hat that fits over my short hair and almost reaches to my eyebrows. Marcus says, "You're cute in that, Katy. I need to give you some red roses to go with that hat."

I can feel the blush covering me. Inwardly, I'm shouting, "He called me cute. He called me cute!"

"Me?"

"Oh, yes, you're my bright star of Lexington." His hand slides over my breasts. I can barely suppress my sudden and powerful urge to wrap my arms around him and bring my mouth to his.

Two weeks pass. I'm drifting in a warm safe place. I will never settle with Marcus into a humdrum existence. My passion will last forever. Once the movie is running, I look at him and feel his desire rising to meet my own. My fingers play the organ automatically.

Once I miss a cue and come in late. Once I play the wrong chords. Twice the house manager speaks to me. But when the movie is on, and the audience is lost in Charlie Chaplin, I belong to Marcus.

When he brushes the back of his hand across my cheek at unexpected moments, I can feel it leap to his touch. I sing as I bike now. On Sunday, I take mother out to dinner because I will probably be leaving her soon. We have Breast of Chicken a la Rose, Waldorf salad, Mayonnaise, and Venetian Ice Cream. She eats every morsel, although she refuses to call it "breast of chicken"—ladies don't use that word, she tells me.

That Monday, we are changing the film to *The Freshman,* a comedy film about a nerdy college freshman, who is trying to become popular by joining the school football team. His only real friend is Peggy, who, according to the subtitles, is "what your mother was like when she was young." At the end, she tells him that she loves him. I love that scene.

Marcus comes in carrying one yellow rose. "For me?" I ask.

"For goodbye."

What is he saying?

He nods. "I am leaving town today. Time to get back to my wife and family."

"Your what…?"

"My family, Katy. I've been doing some work here, but it's time for me to go."

I nod dumbly. He's leaving me. He can't. He was teasing me. I stare into his face as he brushes the hair back from my eyes.

He grabs me, kissing me hard. "It's been great, Katy." And he walks out.

It was never real! It was just another romance—like in my books. If I had been more sophisticated, maybe I would have realized that he was just toying with me, but my only knowledge of romance came from my films and books with their 'happily ever after' endings. There wasn't going to be one of those for me. Ever.

I stand up from my bench. The newsreels haven't run yet. I have time. I run up the stairs to the kitchen, turn on the oven, kneel down, and put my head in. It is *The End*.

Movie theaters are perfect places for ghosts. There they can live out the rest of their story. When an employee is all alone in the Lexington Flick, he or she often feels a presence, hears someone walking, opening and shutting doors or notices some other sounds that don't fit with an empty theater. He or she then knows that Katy is on the prowl. Katy is often seen, dressed in white, floating up the stairs to the abandoned dressing room. Legend has it that she breaks machinery, but perhaps an accident-prone employee spread that rumor. When the employees held a séance in 1987, however, they heard noises in response to their calls.

Historic Lexington Theater

Felix Viano and his wife Theresa emigrated from Italy. By 1916, Felix owned several homes and several buildings on Massachusetts Avenue. He opened The Lexington Theater on January 20, 1917, donating its opening night profits for a benefit for the proposed Lexington gym. His ownership of the theater led to the names of neighboring businesses: Theatre Pharmacy and Theatre Camera. He was a successful man.

The theater's conversion to sound happened in the 1930s. It maintained its organ, which had originally provided the theater with its only sound, until the late 1960s.

Today, Lexington Flick is a small, homey two-screen theater on Massachusetts Avenue. As one website says, it's nothing special architecturally, except that it is one of the very few suburban town center cinemas still operating in this part of the country. Before the theater was a "Flick," it spent several years as part of the Sack Theatres. Throughout its life, it always had shown films for children and senior citizens.

Twenty years later, a new owner bought the old rectory and found the same gilt-framed picture. They decided to hang the picture, and suddenly windows open and shut, doorbells rang and no one was there. When they put it away, all was quiet. They had never heard the story above until I called them . Now, we know there's a ghost for sure!

Historic Brick Parsonage

The brick parsonage was probably the first brick house built in Lexington in the early nineteenth century. It was the honeymoon cottage of Nathaniel Harrington. In 1925, Elizabeth Harrington willed it to the town, which sold it to the Church of Our Redeemer. Architect William Rodger Greeley restored it for the church.

Legends are stories that have been passed down through the generations. Often, they are presented as history, but that may not be necessarily true. They are believable, but not necessarily believed. After all, are there really curses, visions of one's death, or evil spirits? Who knows ...

Part Two
LEGENDS

The Spirit of the Springs

ong before the Europeans began exploring North America, the Indians ruled the land. They lived within its beauty—rather than changing it to meet their needs. They didn't take saws and axes to the forests, plant fields, or establish themselves as farmers. They didn't establish permanent communities or laws regarding how people lived. They didn't disrupt the way of life in the wilderness.

In the northern corner of the Town of Bedford were three, never-failing springs of pure water and a lovely little pond. Fish swarmed in its waters. Animals came down from the forest to drink from the crystal clear springs. The medicine men from the Nipmuck and Pawtucket tribes frequented the site's springs and encouraged their sick and ailing to drink these waters.

A lovely Native American woman, called Naomai, lived in a Nipmuck village near the pond with her husband and daughter. Their life was a happy one. Her husband would bring down moose, deer, and even bear with his bow and arrow. She would run along the trail behind her husband with her baby on her back. Sometimes she would join him in fishing for perch and trout. They would sit for hours while he told her about his adventures when the tribe went on the warpath. In the evening, they would wrap their arms around each other as they listened to the whispering of the pine trees and watched the fireflies flickering in the evening's dusk. Her infant daughter, Rosene, cooed and laughed.

Hurit had been Naomai's best friend since they were little girls. Although Hurit professed to love Naomai, she was very envious of Naomai, who was well liked by all. No one confided in Hurit or asked her join them in their daily activities. Of course, like many of us who never imagined that we could have an enemy disguised as a friend, Naomai didn't realize that her envious friend despised her. One day, Hurit accused her of stealing from the tribe. Naomai laughed at her, thinking she was joking. Hurit just glared at her. Realizing that Hurit was serious, Naomai begged, cried, and pled her innocence, asking, "How can you accuse me? I would never steal."

"But you did, and you are guilty of breaking tribal laws," sneered Hurit, "You deserve to die." The laws of the tribe were harsh, and the village council condemned Naomai to death by water. They planned to tie her in a canoe loaded with rocks and launch it in the lake after they punched holes in it.

All night, Naomai prayed that the Great Spirit would allow her to see her daughter grow up. She just wanted to hold Rozene against her heart one more time.

The next morning, the air was cold and still. Even the villagers were quiet, and the small animals scurried deep into the forest. As the Indians tied Naomai into the rock-filled canoe and placed it into the pond, the rays of the sun shone all around her, creating a golden aura, and a flock of brilliant red cardinals flew about. The Indians were awe struck. Cardinals never came in a flock. Perched on the edge of the canoe, they sang a long beautiful melody. Their reflection turned the water of the lake red. Was Naomai a spirit? The Indians were so frightened that they thrust the canoe into the pond, where it sank. Later, the Indians retrieved the sunken canoe, but much to their astonishment her body had disappeared.

For about a week, some insisted they could see her spirit shimmering in the water. The old women of the tribe told stories about Naomai. They said she was the spirit of the spring, keeping its water crystalline pure. That it was she who offered healing qualities to those tribe members who were ill. Soon Naomai was nothing more than a story that the elders told.

As the years passed, Naomai's baby, Rozene, grew in loveliness. She was so beautiful that Abooksigun, a young, good-looking brave whom no woman could resist, began noticing her. When Abooksigun played his flute, its magic sound hypnotized young women. On hearing it, women would just leave their dwellings and go to Abooksigun, abandoning their families. Of course, after possessing them, he ignored them, leaving them broken hearted.

Naomai, who dwelled in the springs, sensed her child was in trouble. So one day when Rozene came to the spring for water, Naomai leapt up in a great burst of water and brought her down into her watery world. Rozene's father and tribe members looked for her day after day, but she never returned. Finally, a medicine man told them that she was with her mother in the spring. Some believed the medicine man and others didn't. Some said that the voices of these two women could be heard in the spring's gurgling. Others said they could see Rozene's face in the ripples. They all said that the water possessed a magical purity.

During the mid-1800s, one villager told stories about how the Native Americans came to drink and bathe in Bedford Springs. The man who owned the surrounding land furnished pasturage for the villagers' cattle. He noticed that the cattle always went to the springs for water rather than to the open pond. He also saw that the cows with access to the springs were in better condition and gave better milk than those confined in neighboring pastures with better grass.

The water from the springs was analyzed and found to contain health-sustaining minerals. The word spread to Boston. More and more people left the crowded congested streets of the city to enjoy the pastoral scenes and clean air of Bedford. Perhaps they too could become strong. Entrepreneurs built posh hotels; one was the Springs House Hotel, which assumed a spa-like presence as city dwellers began to recognize the advantages of a vacation in a semi rural environment where the air and water were pristine.

In 1856, Dr. William R. Hayden bought the forty-acre property with the Springs House Hotel, stable, bathhouse, and

SOUTH-EAST VIEW. SWEETWATER HOTEL, BEDFORD SPRINGS, MASS.

Postcard courtesy of S. L. Doran; S. Lawrence Whipple, collector

bowling alley. He added beautiful gardens, woodland paths, and summerhouses at the sites of the mineral spring, a narrow gauge railroad, a depot, and a post office. He employed workers who had Spring Pond transformed into Fawn Lake. A beautiful little world surrounded those springs. From near and far, patrons arrived by horse and carriage and railroad. They bathed in the springs, walked on the paths, and enjoyed that vernal setting. Seizing upon the opportunity, Dr. Hayden established his New York Pharmaceutical Company, which served as a bottling plant for approximately 350 healthy drinks based on the spring waters. He also developed several original products: The Compound Phosphorous Pills, The Uric Solvent, and Hayden's Viburnum Compound, which was produced at the rate of 5,000 pounds a year. If the springs didn't make the hotel patrons feel better, perhaps Dr. Hayden's pharmaceuticals would.

By 1891, the resort included about two hundred acres of cleared area and woodland, a large artificial lake with rowboats, a summer hotel, three medicinal springs, railroad

station, and post office. In 1898, the hotel was renamed Hotel Sweetwater.

The years passed. The hotel closed in 1913. The railroad bed was changed into a nature trail. The pharmaceutical products were no longer made, although old bottles are still found; and other uses were found for the pharmaceutical laboratory. In the 1980s, it was converted into a nine-unit residential condominium. The lake no longer reflected the sky, and no one ever saw a flock of cardinals again. But if you sit quietly in the early dawn, you can hear one or two cardinals singing their magical melody, and when you look into the water, you can sometimes see a beautiful woman.

The Indian's Leap

Levi Doran of the Lexington Historical Society found this poem in a box of papers in the archives of the Lexington Historical Society. The box had no accession numbers, meaning that no record exists about who gave it to the society. He surmises that the event occurred somewhere between 1634-1712 at the ledge just before the intersection of Waltham Street and Marrett Road.

One stormy day a heavy wind
Was heard in mournful lays,
It brought a legend back to me
I heard in boyhood days.
A legend filled with doleful hap
And called "the Indian's leap,"
A tragedy the years have held
Long locked in mem'rys keep.
Before the Waltham road was built
In what was Cambridge Farms
But now the town of Lexington
So rich in nature's charms,
A ledge of rock abrupt at end
Stretched through the forest glade,
It barred the present southward way
To Waltham and its trade.
No Indian tribe found Lexington
Adapted for abode
But further west in Concord Town
Its wigwams thickly showed,
Thence thither to the Salty Bay
An Indian trail straight led
Its course passed through sweet Lexington
And o'er its warriors sped.
One day a band of white men spied

An Indian maid alone
And for the maiden made close chase
And now begins my moan:
The maiden from the trail swift turned
To seek another route,
Far through the forest sped her steps,
The white men in pursuit.
At last the forest opened wide
She saw the ledge appear
Along its crest she swiftly sped
The white men closely near,
Despair had seized the Indian's heart
She gave a sudden leap
And from the ledge to vale below
She landed in a heap

They found her at the rocks steep end
The spirit in her gone,
Her neck was broken in the fall
They buried her at more
Quite oft' at dusk a shade is seen
To cross the ledge and weep,
The maiden's soul is bidden there
To haunt "The Indian's Leap."

—Archive of Lexington Historical Society
—not accessioned

The Witch of Shawsheen

s the trickle of settlers moving into the back-hill country began to establish themselves, they looked for water mill sites for their forest products and their grain. The small village of Bedford relied on the Bacon-Fitch Mill on the Shawsheen River to grind their grain into flour and their corn into meal. When the Indians burned the mill during King Philip's War, the colonists immediately rebuilt it.

The owner of the mill was a young miller with twinkling blue eyes and a broad back. His name was Benjamin. He never stopped grinding, except on the Sabbath when the other villagers and he went to the meetinghouse. He didn't have the time to stop grinding, because each family in the village brought him their grain to be ground into flour. They came to him—not just because he was a good miller—but also because everyone liked the dashing young bachelor. Girls asked their brothers if they could go with them to take the corn for grinding. Daughters begged to accompany their fathers to the mill. When they arrived at the mill, the young women forgot about the corn and thought only about the blue-eyed miller. They tossed their hair, they smiled winningly, they lifted their eyes to his, but—much to their sorrow—he never seemed to notice them.

Their mothers asked Benjamin to supper, but he pointed out his workload. Their fathers asked him to come after meeting, but he smilingly shook his head.

One spring, Benjamin was missing from the mill for several days. No one had seen him. The young women were alarmed. They had gone all the way to the mill to see him, and he wasn't there. Where could he have gone? Was something wrong?

One farmer had a daughter of marriageable age whom he wanted to get off his hands. He asked the miller's assistant, "Where's the miller?"

The assistant replied. "He visits a friend downstream in Andover."

"You mean Benjamin's not here?" The farmer was dumfounded.

"Well, now that the grass is turning green again and the trees are in bud, Benjamin may have other things on his mind."

For the next several months, the miller would occasionally disappear. When he returned, the villagers noticed that he seemed to joke more often and that his smile was bigger than before.

When the yellow and orange flowers of late August were in bloom, and the bees danced in the warm breezes as they smelled the apples ripening, the pastor announced the marriage banns for Benjamin Fay and Miriam Gray, whose father's home was on the banks of the Shawsheen in Andover. "I publish the banns of marriage between Benjamin Fay of Bedford and Miriam Gray of Andover. If any of you know any cause or just impediment why these two persons should not be joined together in holy matrimony, ye are to declare it. This is the first time of asking."

The young unmarried women of the parish were heartbroken. A woman could warm her hands and heart upon Benjamin's strength and his blue eyes. He would be a good supporter and a grand father of blue-eyed children. They sat in small groups, murmuring unhappily. They agreed that they could have been content if any one of them had succeeded in capturing his heart, but losing him to a stranger was unbearable.

The pastor published the banns on three successive Sundays. The wedding took place in Andover in June. Afterwards, Miriam and Benjamin stepped into their canoe and paddled twenty miles upstream to the miller's landing on the Shawsheen.

The following Sabbath, the bride and her smiling groom arrived at the meetinghouse. She appeared in a scarlet cloak with a bonnet to match, which contrasted smartly with her sparkling dark eyes and her shiny dark hair. She smiled at the congregation and blew a kiss to the little children. There was a universal gasp. The women in the congregation were dressed in subdued grays and browns. Their snug white bonnets covered their hair. Ducking their heads, they began to whisper about her inappropriate attire.

Benjamin reached out a hand and drew her to his side. She smiled into his eyes and patted his cheek. The congregation gasped in horror.

One elderly woman whispered to another, "I heard from a friend in Andover that it was predicted at her birth that Miriam Gray would be a witch."

The other woman cackled, "She certainly looks like one now."

"Maybe she bewitched him," said another woman leaning forward.

"He most certainly acts it."

One jealous daughter snapped, "She's the witch of the Shawsheen."

"Maybe so," said her mother.

The young women who had flirted with Benjamin began to whisper among themselves. "The Witch of Shawsheen, the Witch of Shawsheen."

The word spread; Miriam's neighbors shunned her. No one wanted to be acquainted with a witch. They whispered when she came down the road with her basket. They turned away when she spoke to them, and the little children ran from her. The Shawsheen River dwindled to a brook because of a drought; the mill was silent; the farmers had no way to grind their corn; and water for their cattle became scarce. At meeting, the villagers prayed that the bottles of heaven might be unstopped. Finally, the rains came, but the villagers continued to ostracize her. Miriam helped Benjamin dig the garden and till the field. In the evening, they sat arm in arm, listening to the whispering of the pine trees and watching the fireflies flitting through the evening's dusk.

The corn shriveled up that fall, and worms ate the cabbages. The potatoes were mealy, and the pumpkins died on the vine. The mourning doves sang their low-toned moaning call, *coo, coo, coo, coo,* and the wind murmuring in the trees warned her to leave. But Miriam stayed.

When she walked to the springs, hidden eyes watched her, and some children called her a witch. Several even pointed their fingers at her. Her smile no longer glowed; her eyes didn't sparkle. Even her hair wasn't very shiny any more. She and Benjamin sat quietly in their house, listening to the cawing of the crows.

Then a child in the village became sick with throat distemper. Soon, five more were sick. One woman had two children die, one after another. The village's doctor hoped that bloodletting would cure the next three people who had the disease, but they too died. At meeting, the pastor said that the disease was because of the "Sin of our First Parents" or Adam and Eve. He counseled the citizens to view death as God's punishment for their sinfulness. One woman sobbed out loud, "I don't want to suffer eternal damnation." The meetinghouse bell tolled frequently as death reached into all corners of the village. The woman who had already lost two children now had another very sick child. She was so distraught that all she did was weep, leaving her sick child in misery.

One morning, Miriam packed a bag of useful herbs, some honey, and a bottle of water from the Bedford Springs. She announced to Benjamin that she was going to help the suffering.

"Miriam. They won't let you do that."

"I have to try. I have skills that can help."

Miriam went to the mother whose third child was dying. At first, she resisted. "No, no, you're a witch. "

"If I am a witch, I am a good witch," said Meriam. "And I know I can make your child well." The woman looked doubtful, but she let Meriam in. Meriam made the mother rest and put her hands on the child's head. "You will be well now. You will see." Then she gave the child a drink made from the herbs, the honey, and the water from the springs.

When the child woke up, she smiled. "I feel so much better," she said. Another woman with a sick husband asked Miriam for help. In several weeks, Miriam nursed many of the villagers through the illness, and she was particularly kind to the old woman who had said she was the Witch of the Shawsheen. From then on, the people of Bedford called for her services when they were sick. Whether she used witchcraft or not, they didn't care. They just wanted her to make them well.

The Money Hole

Many of us have looked for buried treasure sometime during our lives. I always wondered about hidden drawers in desks and holes in old trees (Nancy Drew was always finding things there); others dive around shipwrecks; and some still think treasure can be discovered in caves or pits.

According to the Proceedings of the Lexington Historical Society, there once was a shoemaker, William T. Smith. He lived in what was known as "Smith's End," which is off Waltham Street. Although he was not a rich man, his life was a happy one. His business did well—so well that sometimes he employed two or three other people. He and his wife, Cynthia Childs, were happy and healthy. In 1862, they celebrated their golden wedding anniversary, which was a milestone in those days when people did not live as long as they do now. The two of them cared for their family and friends, helped their neighbors, and worked hard. When evening came, they looked at each other over the supper table and smiled with contentment. At night, they slept in each other's arms, both gently snoring.

Not far from their house, down the road, was a large rock, which was said to be near a buried stash of money. The local people called this place, the Money Hole. Some even said that they had seen ghosts hovering about the area. William wondered whether he ought to dig for the treasure, but he was too busy making shoes. Cynthia thought what ease that money could bring to their lives, but she had grandchildren to care for, suppers to make, and laundry to be washed. So they shrugged their shoulders and said they were too busy with life to be yearning after treasure that may or may not be there.

Other villagers did not feel the same way. Nathan Chandler said he would find the treasure. He left his job in the blacksmith's shop and dug for days and found nothing. When he returned to the shop, he no longer had a job. Caleb Wellington told his fiancé that they would get married once he found the treasure, but he dug for two months and found nothing. When he was through, she said she was through with him too. Several others attempted to find the treasure. They dug and dug and found nothing, but while they were busy digging, they lost their good jobs, ignored their family and friends, and spurned their neighbors' entreaties for help.

One neighbor George Adams, said he dug for the money and found an iron pot. Just before he opened the pot, his mother called to him, "George! The cows are in the mire." When he returned, the iron pot had vanished.

People still wonder whether the Money Hole contained gold or perhaps it was a pot of nothing at the end of the road.

Yo Ho Ho at White Pond

Most people think of pirates as the dashing, well-educated sons of upright English families. They are the swashbuckling Robin Hoods of the sea, sporting cocked pistols, eye patches, and cutlasses. They know how to swashbuckle, mop the poop deck, use a cat o'nine tails, and—if they must—walk the plank. Some, like John Hawkins, profited royally from stealing slaves from Portuguese ships off West Africa and selling them illegally all over the Spanish Main. Some, like English-born Blackbeard, chose piracy over unemployment at the end of one of the many European wars. Others, like Rhode Island's Thomas Tew, became successful privateers during Britain's conflict with France and then turned to the excitement of piracy.

Of course, the great riches of the Spanish Main were what lured so many seafarers into the life of a pirate. From the sixteenth to the eighteenth century, the Spanish fleet transported great hoards of gold, silver, gems, spices, hardwoods, leather, and other riches from the New World to Spain. Although these buccaneers are supposed to have wooden sea chests loaded with gold bullion, pieces of eight, and jewels, their treasure was more often hogsheads of sugar, pewter, silverware, bolts of cloth, and other practical necessities from captured merchant ships. The pirate captain sometimes took the whole ship as a prize and forced the captive crew to join them.

Although many pirate stories talk about buried treasure, findings of such treasure are rare according to researchers. The treasure more often ended up at the bottom of the sea or in the pockets of the shop owners in the pirate's favorite ports, such as Port Royal, Jamaica, where they squandered their booty on demon rum, buxom beauties, and twenty-four-hour gambling.

Somehow, Concord seems a long way from pirate captains and treasure chests. To this day, however, many believe that

there is pirate treasure at the bottom of White Pond in Concord
—thanks to Henry David Thoreau.

In one journal entry for November 5, 1854, he left behind
an interesting, although confusing, story that has inspired many
to seek missing pirate treasure.

According to Thoreau's entry, he and Charles Wheeler were
boating on White Pond in Concord when John Hosmer and
Anthony Wright called them over. The latter two men wanted
Thoreau and Wheeler to see where they had been digging for
treasure. Thoreau reported that he saw a hole six feet square
and six feet deep. Hosmer said the same hole was dug up two
or three weeks before—that three men came in a carriage and
dug it in the night. He went on to say the men had been seen
there by day and someone had dug there earlier. For more
than a hundred years, according to Hosmer, people had been
digging in this area looking for this treasure.

When Thoreau asked for more details about this ancient
treasure trove, Hosmer said that old Mr. Wood, who lived near
him, told him the following story. One night in Captain Kidd's
day, several desperate-looking men asked permission to bury
deerskin breeches filled with coins in Mr. Wood's cellar. Afraid,
he turned them down, and, instead, lent them some earthen
pots, shovels, and a lantern. A woman in the house followed
the trio for a distance, but then she became scared and hurried
home. Later, the men returned the tools and gave Mr. Wood
a hat full of coins. Initially, he buried it in his cellar, but then,
since he was a poor man—and money is money—he dug it up
and spent it.

Still later, storytellers assure us that the deerskin breeches
filled with treasure are in the depths of White Pond—just
awaiting discovery by the right person. In fact, people still
come to the Concord Library to get directions.

Ghostly Guardians
of the Muzzey Homestead

S. Levi Doran tells a story about the Muzzeys, who were among the first settlers of Cambridge Farms (the earlier name for Lexington) about 1642. They built their first house on the lot at the corner of Grant Street and Massachusetts Avenue. In the mid-1700s, they replaced it with another, which was pillaged by the British soldiers on April 19, 1775. In the mid 1830s, that house was moved and again replaced. Around the turn of the twentieth century, the Edison Station purchased the lot and the Muzzeys moved that house to Glen Road Extension.

Many Muzzeys, who were prominent members of local society, lived in the grand mansion. Benjamin Muzzey brought the railroad to Lexington in the 1840s, for instance, forever changing the character of the town. Finally, in the 1970s, only one Muzzey was left: Clifford, Jr. When he was almost eighty, he caught pneumonia and realized that he could no longer function in the house, which had no central heating, and was also lacking in several other modern "necessities."

Clifford sold the family mansion to John Oberteuffer and Kathy Mockett, who still reside there. When they moved in, they also purchased separately from Clifford the majority of the old family artifacts and heirlooms, which were still in the house: a vast treasure trove of a collection, and a doorway into years past. Of course, Clifford wished to take a few items with him.

One day, the neighbors took Clifford back to his old home, to pick up one of the last loads of his belongings. They waited on the second floor landing, while he went up to the attic for a final look. Everything seemed normal, until they heard shouting from above. Clifford was having a heated argument with…. no one. That is, no one living. He was addressing his beloved older sisters, who had all predeceased him many years before. Apparently, Annie, Susie, and Bessie were accusing him of selling off the old house and a majority of family possessions, without good reason. Cliff was replying that there was no other way, and that he had to sell.

Soon after they began to call 14 Glen Road South their home, Kathy and John heard two windows shaking violently. They went to investigate; these windows, which were the only two of that style in the house, were rattling in their frames very insistently. They looked up into the sky: no airplanes. They looked out onto the street: no trucks or cars nearby. There was no one stomping on the floor upstairs. So, "who could it be?" they asked themselves.

This disturbing phenomenon reoccurred many times over the next few months. Exactly one year after it began, however, this occurrence stopped and never happened again.

The only explanation for this phenomenon is that Clifford's long-dead sisters were concerned that Kathy and John might disrespect what the sisters still considered their home. Also, most of the old furniture was still in the house. The sisters probably felt invaded when newcomers entered their long-cherished home. Over the course of that first year however, Annie, Susie, and Bessie learned that Kathy and John respected their family heirlooms, and above all, the structure which their forebears and themselves had called "home" for a century and a half.

The three sisters know that Kathy and John will preserve their family's heritage and treat everything with care. Now, they have accepted the new residents of their home.

Part Three
LORE

*I*n ages past, our grandparents were the storytellers. This was the way things were passed through the generations that followed. Their tales were part of our heritage. They were ones we all know—that we have grown up with.

The English Way of Life

Massachusetts Bay Colony was a formidable wilderness. For centuries, the American Indians enjoyed their great unspoiled valleys and lakes. The Indian braves hunted the land and fished the water, leaving planting and other domestic tasks to their women. The land could easily sustain them because the American Indians cleared only the land they needed to survive. With their insatiable appetite for territory, however, the colonists took axes and saws to the wilderness, converting the woodlands to farmland and establishing frontier communities and rules of law, religion, and property ownership. The colonists also worked to convert the Indians to Christianity. Those who became converted were known as "praying Indians."

Founded in 1635, the six-mile square Town of Concord was located at the junction of the Concord/Sudbury/Assabet Rivers. Some twenty miles northwest of Boston, the frontier outpost was mainly farmland or woodlot.

Initially, the English labored to convert and improve the natives. The differences between the English and the native cultures soon caused friction. The colonists assumed the American Indians would adopt the English farming, shepherding, housing, legal, and religious practices. Many of the natives resented the settlers' rules, arrogance, and their relentless acquisition of land. The settlers acquired and fenced more land, grew more crops, and raised more livestock, putting increased pressure on traditional Indian hunting and planting practices. The English were in the New World to stay, and the wilderness was slowly disappearing. Ultimately, tensions led to the bloodiest war in American colonial history, King Philip's War, in 1675-1676. Approximately eight hundred settlers and three thousand natives died.

This is where my story begins. Let me introduce myself. I am John Hoar, a Concord resident, who lives on Lexington Road. I was born in Britain and trained as a lawyer.

In 1675, because of the Indian raids, the Massachusetts General Court decided that they could not trust the Christian Indians and began to intern them, although they had remained loyal to the Crown. The authorities removed the inhabitants from the praying towns of Natick and Ponkapog to Deer Island, located in Boston Harbor. Near Concord was a village of Nashoba Indians, who had deliberately adopted English customs as part of their conversion to Christianity. They wore European clothes and cut their hair short, used English metal tools and blankets, and sometimes worked as laborers for the settlers. However, they still hunted for food and furs and lived in wigwams.

Because of the food and fuel shortage in Nashoba, the General Court persuaded our Concord selectmen to intern the fifty-eight Nashoba Indians in our town. Many of my neighbors were terrified and furious; how could they possibly trust the natives? There was no way, according to some, that a white English-bred settler could live cheek by jowl with a Nashoba Indian—whether he was a Christian or not—not in our lovely little town! But the Court had so decreed, and the town faced a dilemma.

So I said I would assume the responsibility. Generally, I am well respected, although I have been admonished for criticizing the quality of Massachusetts's justice and for missing meeting. These Puritan communities believe in the strict and decorous observance of Sunday. Sabbath breaking is not tolerated!

Despite my defilement of the Lord's Day, the town gratefully accepted my offer to house the fifty-eight Nashoba Indians, these twelve braves, their women, and children, on my land. I built them a workhouse and residence and instructed and protected this group of "praying Indians." Naïve that I was, I thought everything was going fine.

My neighbors were far from pleased. Some called on that bow-legged scoundrel, Captain Samuel Moseley, who is known to despise the Indians. He was well pleased to be asked to do something about the Indian situation.

On a February Sunday, Captain Mosely and his militiamen went to the meetinghouse. Of course, despite the earlier reprimand, I wasn't there. At the end of the worship, the dastardly Captain declared to the congregation that he understood that there were some heathen in town committed to my care. He announced that he and his militia would remove them to Boston. As happens in these situations, most of the mealy-mouthed people who had just listened to a long sermon about "loving thy neighbor" didn't speak up. The Indians weren't natives after all, they said to themselves, so why should they do anything? Seizing on their apathy, the Captain took their silence for consent. After the meeting was dismissed, he and his militia came to my house on Lexington Road and arrogantly demanded to see the Indians under my care. Like a flock of sheep, the 100 or so men, women, and children who had attended meeting followed along, saying nothing.

I opened the door of the shelter so that everyone there could see that the natives were safely ensconced. Captain Moseley announced, "I have a corporal and soldiers to secure them."

Drawing myself up, I retorted, "There is no need for that. By order of the General Court, I am responsible for keeping and securing them."

The Captain scowled and marched off, but he left his corporal and soldiers there. They proceeded to verbally abuse my charges despite my remonstrations. The next morning Captain Moseley returned, insisting that I surrender the Indians. I stood by my legal training. "I won't deliver them, unless you show me an order from the Court."

The Captain had no such order, but he did have the militia. Bullying his way in, he commanded the corporal to break open the door. They did so, and the people watched, saying nothing. Some soldiers plundered their clothing and household items, and the people watched, saying nothing. Once the Captain had taken the Indians away, the people, my neighbors, quickly assumed control of the Indian lands on the Nashoba plantation. Was this why they had stood there like sheep? Was this their reason for saying nothing when the Captain defied the rule of the Court? Was this why they let the militia plunder the natives' goods?

A guard of twenty men brought the Indians to Charlestown. Ultimately, Captain Mosely was rebuked for his arbitrary action, but nonetheless the Indians were sent to Deer Island to pass into the furnace of affliction with their brethren. Despite all our talk about treating them like Christians—which they were by the way—they were not compensated for their lost food, clothing, and household goods. Nor was I ever paid for the building that I had built for them.

During the winter of 1676, the Nashaway Indians attacked the town of Lancaster and captured Mary Rowlandson, the wife of a Puritan minister and the mother of three, Joseph, Mary, and Sarah. For almost three months, she was hostage to the Indians, witnessing the murder of her friends and the death of one of her children, and suffering starvation and depression. Despite what had happened in Concord, both the Indians and settlers trusted me so much so that I successfully negotiated Mary Rowlandson's release.

Life is made up of many converging currents—both good and bad. I was well pleased when I could pay Mary Rowlandson's ransom of twenty pounds to the Indians at Redemption Rock in Princeton. But I couldn't do anything about those Nashoba Indians, many of whom died on Deer Island deprived of adequate food or shelter. Perhaps it is for this reason that I rarely attend Sunday meeting.

The Case of the Forgotten Trunk

Early in the morning of April 19, 1775, —just as the British column could be seen in the distance—John Hancock's clerk, John Lowell, remembered that he had left Hancock's trunk at Buckman Tavern in Lexington. It contained Hancock's correspondence and papers from the Provincial Congress and Committee of Safety that could incriminate many Rebel leaders. Panicked, he approached Paul Revere, who was walking back into town, and the two men hurried towards Buckman Tavern with its prominent chimneys and gambrel roof.

On the common, drummer William Diamond was beating the call to muster. Some militia were still sitting in the taproom, debating what this alarm meant. Revere told them that yes, indeed, the British were coming, and could even be seen to the east advancing towards the Common. The militia ran outside; Revere and Lowell headed upstairs to the rear second floor room where the six-foot-long leather-covered trunk was stored. Lugging the heavy box down the narrow stairs, they exited out the front door of the tavern and onto the town Common.

There, Orderly Sergeant Munroe had about forty militia in line. Others were milling about, running back to the tavern for their ammunition or coming across the meadow and pasture that cold gray April dawn. By now, the British Regulars stood, waiting for orders from their officers. Women and children peered from behind houses. As all this was happening, Revere and Lowell proceeded to carry their heavy burden full of incriminating papers across the Common, through the militia's lines. Luckily for everyone concerned, nobody stopped them. Revere and Lowell carted the trunk into the woods just outside of town. It was safe from the British.

Later, Revere would recall that he did not see the first shot fired, but he heard it:

> *When we got about 100 yards from the meeting-House the British Troops appeared on both Sides... I saw and heard a Gun fired... Then I could distinguish two Guns, and then a Continual roar of Musquetry (sic); Then we made off with the Trunk.*

The irony of it is that after all of Revere's heroics of the night before, the morning of the shot that was heard around the world, he was reduced to carrying a piece of luggage!

Historic Patriots Day

In 1969, the third Monday of April in the states of Maine and Massachusetts was officially designated as Patriots Day. In 1971, in preparation for the Bicentennial, the Lexington Minutemen established themselves as reenactors. The unique aspect of their work is that they each do a first person interpretation of someone who fought on the Lexington green in 1775. The Lexington Minutemen hold the reenactment every Patriots Day and demonstrate colonial military tactics on summer weekends and special occasions.

In Bedford, there is a liberty pole capping. In Concord, on the preceding Saturday, re-enactors march down the trail towards Hartwell Tavern for tactile demonstrations. On Patriots Day in Concord, the parade goes over the bridge, and there are more tactile demonstrations.

The big event remains the reenactment of the Battle on Lexington Green. And, each year, the case of the missing trunk is re-enacted, and Jonathan Harrington dies at his wife's feet on the steps of his home. Incidentally, the British always win and march on toward Concord.

Liberty Pole

Built about 1710 by Benjamin Kidder, the Fitch Tavern has served as a farmhouse, a tavern from 1766-1808, a school for young ladies, and "an underground railroad" station. Today, it is a private residence on Bedford's Great Road. *Courtesy of D. Peter Lund.*

A liberty pole is a tall wooden pole, which may be surmounted by an ensign or a liberty cap. The custom of raising and capping a liberty pole goes back to the summer of 1765, when militant Bostonians demonstrated against the Stamp Act. In August, they burned two tax officials in effigy from the limbs of an elm tree. This tree, which soon became known as the Liberty Tree, acted as an assembling point for the Sons of Liberty and other patriots. To call a meeting, the colonists would fasten a pole with a red flag tied to it to the tree. Angered British soldiers chopped down Boston's original liberty tree during the winter of 1775-1776. During the same time, liberty poles began appearing in other towns from Newport, Rhode Island, to New York City, New York.

The Town of Bedford holds a liberty pole capping every year. *Courtesy of D. Peter Lund*

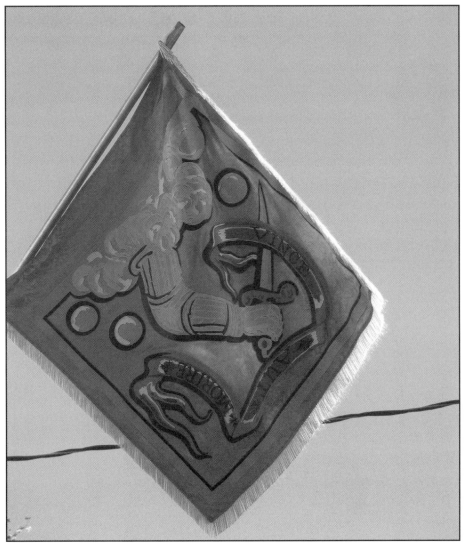

The Bedford Flag is on display at the Bedford Free Public Library. *Courtesy of D. Peter Lund*

Concord's liberty pole stood on a ridge overlooking the town. To punish the defiant colonists, the Regulars chopped down the Concord liberty pole and burned it on April 19, 1775.

Today, on an early Saturday in April, the Bedford Minute Men Company along with other local minute men companies raise a liberty pole capped with a red hat with appropriate music and musket firing.

The Bedford Flag

By 1775, Bedford had many farms and about 470 residents. The town had allotted a portion of its local militia to "minute man status." On the morning of April 19, 1775, following the alarm that the British were on the march from Boston, twenty-six minute men gathered at Fitch Tavern. Captain Jonathan Wilson looked at his men and said, "It is a cold breakfast, boys, but we'll give the British a hot dinner; we'll have every dog of them before night." The Bedford Minute Men then marched to Concord, joining with the fifty men of the Bedford militia on route. One of the first groups to arrive at Old North Bridge, they participated in the battle.

Nathaniel Page of the Bedford Minute Men carried the company standard into battle. Supposedly, the flag was first used by a cavalry troop of the Massachusetts Bay militia during the French and Indian Wars. Many sources consider it to be the oldest American flag still in existence. So far it is known as the first flag carried by the colonials into the battle of North Bridge.

Designed in England sometime between 1660-1670, the almost square piece of red silk damask with a silver and gold design shows the arm of God reaching down from the clouds, with a short sword in a mailed fist on a crimson background. Its Latin motto reads, "Vince aut Morire" (Conquer or Die).

The story is told that, after the battle, it was brought home and stored in an attic. Originally, it had fringe, but in the early 1800s, one of the women in the household needed to adorn her dress. Hence, no more fringe!

Keeping the New World New

Each town should have a park, or rather a primitive forest, of five hundred or a thousand acres, where a stick should never be cut for fuel, a common possession forever, for instruction and recreation... All Walden Wood might have been preserved for our park forever, with Walden in its midst...

—Thoreau's Journal. October 15, 1859

When the original settlers arrived, they were confronted with heavily forested country. If the space was open, it was either water or marshland. Two centuries later, only eleven percent of the land remained wooded. In some areas, soil erosion caused by over farming had become a problem.

Walden Pond is too small (barely sixty acres) to be a significant body of water, but it is incredibly important in the intellectual and spiritual history of the United States. Thanks to Henry David Thoreau, who wrote *Walden; or Life in the Woods*, a chronicle of his two years of "deliberate living" in a small cabin on the pond's northeast shore more than 150 years ago, the pond has become one of the sacred icons of the environmental movement.

When I first paddled a boat on Walden, it was completely surrounded by thick and lofty pine and oak woods and in some of its coves grape vines had run over the trees next to the water and formed bowers under which a boat could pass.

—Thoreau, *Walden*, Chapter 9

The Mass of Men Lead Lives of Quiet Desperation

At a time in the history of our country when there was so much open land that it was unappreciated, Walden Pond had always attracted commerce. One of the first Concord industries

Walden Pond. *Courtesy of Siobhan Theriault*

Statue of Thoreau and the replica of his hut. *Courtesy of Siobhan Theriault*

involved raking up the layer of bog iron ore that lay under the meadows and transporting it in carts to smelters. The smelting, of course, required huge quantities of charcoal, which meant that the charcoal-makers stripped the woods of anything they could transform into charcoal in their earth-covered mounds. They left behind circles of charred earth and the smelting facilities.

The pond was also the site of a pottery work. Concord's slaves and housemaids lived on its shores, as did the immigrant Irish laborers who built the railroad.

By 1844, the Fitchburg Railroad had reached Concord. A stone throw's from the pond, the trains reached Boston in one hour instead of the bumpy three hours required by the stagecoach. Those Concord farmers, who realized that their economic interests were best served by this faster access to the city, now had a readily available market for dairy products and perishable fruits and vegetables. Soon, a milk car was added to the morning train, and Concord's dairy industry thrived.

By 1846, ice cutting, one of the major business enterprises in nineteenth century Boston, came to Walden Pond. Beginning in 1826, Frederic Tudor and his brother decided to start a business in ice trading. Cold winters created ice in ponds such as Walden. The Tudor Brothers decided to "harvest" this ice and sell it to such places as India, Singapore, Havana, and New Orleans, thus earning a tidy profit. Hundreds of Irish laborers commuted from Cambridge by railroad to harvest as much as a thousand tons of ice a day. The ice was stored besides the tracks in straw-insulated piles up to thirty-five feet high. Lying in bed in his hut, Thoreau could hear "the shrill whistle of the steam engine…"

Despite advancing civilization, fishermen and woodcutters still visited the 102-foot deep kettle-hole pond in the 1840s. A twenty-seven-year-old former schoolteacher with deep reservations about the city as a way of life, Henry David Thoreau moved into his one-room cabin at Walden Pond on July 4, 1845. When Thoreau took up residence at Walden that year, much of the pond's shoreline was bare, but he could still boast, "I have my horizon bounded by woods all to myself." There, surrounded by nature, he began to explore the relationship between humanity and nature and people's relationship with each other. Alert to the fleeting beauty of the natural world, Thoreau could hear the cracking of the ice in the pond and the scrabble of squirrels on his roof. On April 18, Thoreau wrote, "I get up early and bathe in the pond—that is one of the best things I do."

Things Do Not Change; We Change

In 1866, the Fitchburg Railroad built an excursion park at Ice Fort Cove on the pond. Many conventions gravitated to the concession stands, swings, bathhouses, boats, dining and dancing hall, and cinder track for runners and bicyclists. Thousands of people visited this once-idyllic spot.

In 1896, fire destroyed one thousand acres surrounding the pond. Edward Emerson wrote, "The shores of our beautiful pond have been devastated by fire and moths and rude and reckless visitors." The excursion park burned down in 1902.

The Town of Concord began offering swimming lessons in 1913, and more than 2,000 visitors a day came to the park. Bathhouses were built in 1917. In 1922, the Emerson, Forbes, and Heywood families granted approximately eighty acres surrounding the pond to the Commonwealth of Massachusetts with the stipulation of "preserving the Walden of Emerson and Thoreau, its shores and nearby woodlands for the public who wish to enjoy the pond, the woods and nature, including bathing, boating, fishing and picnicking." Middlesex County was given the responsibility for management of the reservation.

We hear of cow-commons and ministerial lots, but we want men-commons and lay lots, inalienable forever. Let us keep the New World new, preserve all the advantages of living in the country. There is meadow and pasture and wood-lot for the town's poor. Why not a forest and huckleberry field for the town's rich?

—Thoreau's Journal: October 15, 1859

Thoreau's birth house on Virginia Road in Concord is currently being restored. *Courtesy of Siobhan Theriault*

As the area grew and development advanced, the heirs of Emerson and Thoreau carried on a largely successful campaign to preserve the woods "for our park forever with Walden in its midst." Walden Pond has been designated a National Historic Landmark and is considered the birthplace of the conservation movement. Today, the Department of Environmental Management in cooperation with the Towns of Concord and Lincoln is responsible for the conservation land.

Visitors arrive from dawn to dusk, to swim, to picnic, to play with children along the beach edge. They come in all seasons to walk the trails once walked by Thoreau. Those who come after hours often talk about seeing a strange man staring at the stars or watching the animals of the night—the skunks, raccoons, and red foxes. Sometimes on those early foggy mornings, you might glimpse Thoreau swimming at dawn, watching the chickadees, or marveling at the sky, "whose bottom is pebbly with stars." Those still pond waters offer his belief in living each season as it passes; breathing the air, drinking the drink, tasting the fruit, and resigning yourself to the influences of each.

Walden Pond State Reservation is located at 915 Walden Street/Route 126 in Concord, Massachusetts. The park entrance and parking areas are located across the street from the pond. A replica of Thoreau's cabin is located across the street from the pond near the parking area in the state park; a trail leads to the actual location of Thoreau's cabin, which overlooked the pond.

Thoreau's ghost still hovers over the Concord area. People even refer to the beautiful town as Thoreau's Concord. The only Transcendentalist who was born in Concord, he lived in many different homes there, including the Colonial Inn.

Abolition in Concord

Slavery has been part of the social and economic fiber of America since the first colonists arrived from England. The United States Constitution designates slaves as "all other persons," and they were counted in the census as three-fifths of a free person. By the late eighteenth century, as those who were involved in slavery increased, so did their opponents. By the 1830s, the abolitionist movement became a crusade. Although many Northerners viewed slavery as wrong, they perceived abolition as a threat to their wealth and the social order.

In 1831, the articulate William Lloyd Garrison founded *The Liberator* in Boston, Massachusetts, a newspaper dedicated to the abolitionist movement. Garrison argued for "immediate and complete emancipation of all slaves" and labeled slave-holding a crime. Subsequent abolitionist activities provoked widespread hostile responses from both the North and South. Then the abolitionists began to disagree among themselves. These activities had a significant impact on political and cultural life.

Beginning in 1829, Concord residents were enjoying the many speakers who came to their newly founded lyceum. Experts talked about honeybees, the Siege of Quebec, the life of Plato, capital punishment, and temperance. With men like Ralph Waldo Emerson and David Henry Thoreau living in town, Concord attracted the best speakers of the time. During the lyceum's first fifty years, over 784 lectures were given. By 1836, the prominent men of the town such as Emerson, Alcott, and Thoreau were focusing on transcendentalism, which began as a protest against the general state of culture and society at the time and a belief in the power of the divine and individual messages.

Although the Concord residents were against slavery, many believed the abolitionists were too extreme. The finest minds of Concord were also preoccupied with defining spirituality in relation to the natural world and creating a uniquely American body of literature. It was the women in their lives who took up the abolitionist flag.

Sweet Cakes and Fairs

On October 18, 1837, sixty-one women met at the Concord home of Susan Barrett for the first formal meeting of the newly organized Concord Female Anti-Slavery Society, which focused on sponsoring antislavery speakers and periodicals, raising funds, and improving the lives of the few African Americans in their community. Its leading members included Sophia and Helen Thoreau (Henry's sisters), Lidian Emerson (Ralph Waldo's wife), and Mary Merrick Brooks. One of their missions was to convert both Emerson and his protégé Thoreau to the abolitionist cause.

From the group's inception, they met in each other's homes (much like today's League of Women Voters or garden club meetings) to discuss, strategize, and communicate. As has been true in church fairs for years, they used their domestic talents to raise money for the abolitionist cause. They sold children's clothing, bags, caps, toys, paintings, engravings, and books at anti-slavery fairs. They sold ice cream and other delicacies, offered music, and invited "friends of the slave in Lexington, Littleton, Sudbury, Carlisle, Westford, and all the neighboring towns to attend." They even charged admission. Each year Concord women supplied handcrafted goods and helped to staff the annual Boston anti-slavery fair, which was the country's largest abolitionist fundraiser. The funds raised were used for publications and conventions and to support antislavery agents.

One of the most formidable women was Mary Merrick Brooks. She sold a rich and buttery cake with a lovely golden brown crust made from her own recipe. Together with other Concord women, including Abigail Alcott, Lydian and Ellen

Emerson, Harriet Stowe, and Cynthia and Sophia Thoreau, she arranged teas and dancing parties, where she served her famous Brooks Cake.

While Mary Merrick Brooks was cooking her cakes, she and other members of the society were using their charms to convince some of the country's most noted intellectuals to take a public stand against slavery. In 1844, she persuaded Ralph Waldo Emerson to denounce slavery. Although the town selectmen refused to ring the Town House bell summoning people to hear Emerson's speech, Thoreau rang it anyway. Later, Henry Thoreau accompanied Garrison and Wendell Phillips to a rally in 1854. Their participation lent strength to the abolitionist cause not only in New England but also throughout the country.

John Brown

Abolitionist leaders such as Wendell Phillips, William Lloyd Garrison, and Frederick Douglass visited Concord frequently. In January 1857, John Brown came to town to raise money so that what he called his Holy War against slavery could continue. A clandestine group of wealthy abolitionists, known as the "Secret Six," funded Brown, allowing him to raise a small army. The six included Unitarian minister and friend of Emerson, Theodore Parker, and Concord schoolmaster, Franklin Sanborn. In March, John Brown visited Concord as Sanborn's guest and met Henry Thoreau, who became an ardent admirer. During this visit, Brown spoke against slavery at the Concord Town Hall. Many people in the audience supported him.

Two years later, Brown returned to solicit funds again and to lecture at Town Hall. He raised more funds, which he used to raid the federal arsenal at Harpers Ferry, West Virginia. Robert E. Lee and his troops prevented him from carrying out his plan and killed or captured most of Brown's men. Brown himself was taken to Charlestown, Virginia, where he was tried and convicted of treason, conspiracy, and murder. Subsequently, he was hung.

Brooks Cake*

1 lb flour, sifted
1 lb sugar
½ lb butter, softened
4 eggs at room temperature
1 cup milk
1 teaspoon soda
½ teaspoon cream of tartar
½ lb currants

* **Note:** For today's taste add ½ tsp salt and 1 tsp vanilla.

1. Preheat oven to 350 degrees F and place rack in center of oven.

2. Butter or spray, a 9" x 5" x 3" loaf pan.

3. Line the bottom of the pan with parchment paper and butter or spray the paper. Set aside while you prepare the batter.

4. In a large bowl, sift together the flour and cream of tartar. Set aside.

5. Mix the baking soda in the cup of milk.

6. In the bowl of your electric mixer, or with a hand mixer, beat the butter until creamy and smooth. Gradually add the sugar, beating continuously on medium-high speed until light and fluffy (this will take about 5 minutes). Scrape down the sides of the bowl as needed.

7. After about five minutes, the batter should be light in color and fluffy in texture. Then add the eggs, one at a time, mixing well after each addition. Scrape down the sides of the bowl as needed.

8. Add the flour mixture alternately with the milk mixture and mix just until incorporated.

9. Stir in the currants. Pour the batter into the prepared pan and smooth the top.

10. Bake for about 50 to 60 minutes or until the cake is golden brown and a toothpick inserted in the center comes out clean.

11. Remove the cake from the oven and place on a wire rack to cool for about 10 minutes.

12. Remove the cake from the pan and cool completely.

13. Serve warm or at room temperature.

Although initially shocked by Brown's exploits, some Northerners spoke favorably of the militant abolitionist. "He did not recognize unjust human laws, but resisted them as he was bid," said Henry David Thoreau in an address to the citizens of Concord, Massachusetts. "No man in America has ever stood up so persistently and effectively for the dignity of human nature...." Ralph Waldo Emerson said that Brown was "the rarest of heroes, a pure idealist, with no by-ends of his own." Not all Concordians agreed.

Underground Railroad

Members of Concord's society also supported the Underground Railroad, a dangerous activity. If an individual aided a fugitive slave, they were breaking state and federal laws while the escaping slave was also breaking laws. If captured, the fugitive slave was returned to bondage. Arrested conductors often faced heavy fines. A loosely constructed network of escape routes that began in the South, the Underground Railroad depended on antislavery sympathizers, secret codes, signals, and temporary havens. The runaways seldom had any plans and had little food or clothing. They would travel at night and hide during the daytime. The stationmasters would provide food and shelter and transport to the next station. Thoreau often escorted the fugitives to the West Fitchburg station to board a train for points north.

Researchers believe that from late December 1846 through mid-January 1847 and later in February, Abigail and Bronson Alcott harbored at least one, and possibly two, fugitive slaves in their home, which is now called (thanks to Hawthorne) The Wayside. In a December entry, Abigail comments:

Opposite: For the centennial on April 19, 1875, the town of Concord commissioned Daniel Chester French to create a statue of a Minute Man for approximately $1,000. French's first full-size statue, it stands on a base inscribed with the first verse from Ralph Waldo Emerson's "Concord Hymn." Daniel Chester French went on to create the Lincoln Memorial statue in Washington D.C. *Courtesy of Paul E. Doherty*

The Wayside House was originally the home of Samuel Whitney, muster master of the Concord militia during the Revolution. Mrs. Whitney and her children watched the British march by the house on their way to search for contraband in the town. During the literary renaissance of the nineteenth century, the house became home to: Bronson Alcott, his family and his famous daughter Louisa May; Nathaniel Hawthorne and his wife; and the Lothrops. The Wayside now belongs to the Minuteman Man National Historical Park. *Courtesy of D. Peter Lund*

...this month has been full of interest… the arrival of a Slave named for the present John—an intimate in my family until some place where work can be provided—An amiable intelligent man Just 7 weeks from the 'House of Bondage.

Later in January, she commented that a fugitive slave has been sent on his way. Then on February 2, Bronson writes that a Maryland fugitive has arrived. A week later, he comments that after a week of sawing and piling wood, the fugitive is on his way to Canada. Bronson describes this fugitive as "scarce thirty years of age, athletic, dexterous, sagacious, and self-relying"; he regards his family's hospitality to the slave as "an impressive lesson to my children, bringing before them the wrongs of the black man."

Situated on 455 Lexington Road in Concord, The Wayside is the only National Historic Landmark lived in by three literary families: Alcott family, Nathaniel Hawthorne, and Margaret Sidney, creator of the *Five Little Peppers*, and her daughter, Margaret. In 2001, The Wayside was designated a part of the National Underground Railroad Network to Freedom. Now part of Minute Man National Historical Park, The Wayside is open May through October.

How Not to Entertain a President

In 1870, Lexington and Concord were small farming villages. Of the two, Lexington was smaller, with a population of less than 2,300. In 1870, both Lexington and Concord began to plan for the centennial celebration of the Battle on Lexington Green and at Old North Bridge in Concord. The Town of Lexington commissioned American sculptors Martin Milmore and Thomas R. Gould to carve Carrara marble statues of John Hancock and Samuel Adams to be unveiled at the celebration. The Concord authorities chose a young, unknown sculptor Daniel C. French to sculpt a Minute Man Statue and decided that the Old North Bridge needed to be rebuilt. In 1873, the Lexington committee invited Concord's Board of Selectmen to join with Lexington in the Centennial Celebration; Concord declined this invitation in March 1874.

Each town thought their celebration should be the first in a series of nationwide celebrations culminating with the adoption of the Declaration of Independence on July 4, 1876. The result was competing celebrations with statues commissioned for the occasion, banquets, celebrities, and mobs of people. Unfortunately, for both towns, the weather did not cooperate. It had snowed on April 13; the north winds had blown; and April 19 was an icy 22-degree day. Despite the cold weather, President Grant, various cabinet secretaries, and many other stalwart officials from the Commonwealth attended both celebrations.

The Celebration in Concord

To celebrate the occasion, Concord built an ornate cedar centennial bridge with two covered half-arbor seating areas on the middle portion to provide rest for the weary. They unveiled Daniel Chester French's seven-foot statue of a minute man who left his plow to grab his gun. They set up two giant tents: a 200- by 85-foot oration tent and a 410- by 85-foot tent to accommodate over 4,000 diners. A religious service at First Parish on Sunday preceded the formal ceremonies on April 19. The Portsmouth, Boston, New York, and Washington Navy Yards had sent vast quantities of flags and bunting, which was used to decorate the public buildings, liberty pole, and principal streets.

Cannon fire awoke the people of Concord at 5:18 am on April 19. Drums soon joined in. Concord expected 20,000 visitors; they received about 50,000. Extra trains chugged into town. Police details arrived, and the flags flew that frigid morning. President Ulysses S. Grant, Vice-President Wilson, three cabinet secretaries, and Speaker of House James C. Blaine had spent the night in Concord. Governors of Vermont, Maine, South Carolina, and Massachusetts were present as were many other dignitaries. They all joined the two-mile procession of cavalry companies, infantry regiments, bands, and veterans. At 11 am, after the Minute Man statue's unveiling, about 4,000 people filled the oration tent, which stood on the spot where the colonial militia had assembled for their march down the hill. Two hundred people sat on a platform, and the rest stood—

Lexington Minuteman. *Courtesy of Peter Lund*

probably very close together to take advantage of the body heat. The Honorable Ebenezer Rockwood Hoar of Concord welcomed everyone, and then the Reverend Mr. Reynolds began to pray. As he prayed, wood began to creak. Boards splintered, and the platform holding the dignitaries collapsed, depositing President Grant and others on the ground. President Grant stood up, and the prayer was completed. The platform was propped up again, but during James Russell Lowell's ode, it collapsed again. When the seventy-two year old Ralph Waldo Emerson spoke, no one could hear him. The audience became noisy until Judge Hoar admonished them to preserve silence.

At the ceremony's end, the President, Vice President, and other dignitaries left for Lexington. Meanwhile, the 4,000 guests had a chilly dinner under the tent while the remaining 50,000 people foraged for food throughout the town. By 2 pm, nothing edible was left in any Concord restaurant or tavern. Famished visitors stormed Middlesex Hotel, but the police threw them out. The selectmen closed the taverns, which sent hungry people to bootleggers. People singing Civil War ballads and reeking of alcohol filled the streets, but there was little disorder. By 6 pm, most of the crowd had gone home, and Concord residents who had invitations enjoyed the Grand Ball in the Middlesex Agricultural Society hall.

The Celebration in Lexington

Lexington also marked historic spots and erected two great tents on the two and one-half acre Lexington Common and a large arc inscribed "Welcome to the Birthplace of America's Liberty" at its entrance. Gas-illuminated, wooden-floored, lavishly decorated tents occupied a large portion of the Common. The 200- by 80-foot pavilion tent was closest to the arch and reached by an evergreen-bowered path. A short covered passage connected the nearby dining tent, which could seat about 3,500 guests, to the pavilion tent. Booths and makeshift restaurants sprung up all over town. Many volunteers, including young women from Cambridge and Arlington, offered to wait tables in the dining tents.

On the chilly Sunday preceding the celebration day, Lexington held its church service and dedicated the statues of John Hancock and Samuel Adams now standing in Cary Memorial Hall. Despite the unseasonably cold weather, large numbers of visitors strolled the streets, visiting historic spots, and even attending the church services. The crowds increased all day.

On April 19, the ceremony commenced at sunrise with a 100-gun salute. Traffic increased steadily; trains with locomotives gaily decked with bunting steamed into Lexington, depositing even more visitors—some of whom had clung to the outer rails or the roof in their desire to be part of the celebration. The ensuing traffic jam was so immense that rail and highway vehicles came to a halt. One hundred thousand people came to the small farming village to participate in the festivities.

Bands played, people hawked their wares, and the crowds milled about, trying to keep warm in the piercing wind. The pavilion tent, which was intended to hold 7,000 people, was open for morning ceremonies. The audience stamped their feet on the wooden floor to keep warm.

No train had passed between Lexington and Concord since the early morning hours. President Grant, his cabinet, and some other dignitaries took a carriage from Concord but were stuck in traffic outside of Lexington while many of the dignitaries had to walk. Meanwhile the Lexington procession waited for them to form the reviewing stand. Learning that the President was stuck in traffic at the west end of town, the red-coated National Lancers rescued the President. Placing him in their grand carriage, they escorted him past the entire procession as it stood waiting. At the end of the parade, the celebrities and those who could pay the $5 fee went to the dinner tent, which had been stormed earlier by the hungry crowds. Little food remained, and the volunteer waitresses were in tears. Despite the cold, a festive ball in the large pavilion to the music of the village band drew an estimated 2,000 people. After an hour of festivities, President Grant planted a young elm tree at the main entrance to the common. Meanwhile, a tired, cold, hungry mob of people surrounded the railroad station hoping to get home. The Lexington citizens opened their doors to strangers on the streets and fed them, while churches offered pews and aisles for overnight guests.

The next years were quieter. In 1894, Patriots Day was declared a state holiday. Lexington erected the memorial to Captain Parker in 1900. In 1911, actors performed the Battle of Lexington on the Common. It was considered a failure because there were too many dogs and children. These days, there are many children, not very many dogs, and lots of cameras.

In 1975, U. S. President Gerald R. Ford visited both Concord and Lexington on the occasion of the Bicentennial. He spoke at the ceremonies on the Lexington Green. That day was warm and sunny and crowded.

Today, the Towns of Lexington and Concord and the Minute Man National Historical Park preserve historic structures and sites from April 19, 1775. By Act of Congress (1965), the American flag flies twenty-four hours a day from a 135-foot flag pole in the center of the Lexington Battle Green as a tribute to those who stood their ground that fateful morning. Concord's Old North Bridge is where the colonials first resisted the British with force. These two New England towns and the road between them have played a major role in the history of the United States and the world.

Bibliography

Andres, Joseph, Jr., *Revolutionary Lexington & Concord*, Concord. MA: Concord Guide Press. 1998.

Bacheller, Carrie. *Munroe Tavern: the custodian's story*. Lexington, Massachusetts: Lexington Historical Society, 19__

Barker, John. *The British in Boston*. New York, NY: Arno Press, 1969.

Blancke. "Concord and Native First People," *In New Perspectives on Concord's History*. Concord, Massachusetts, 1983.

Brenner, Barbara. *If You Were There in 1776*. New York, New York: Bradbury Press, 1994.

Brooks, Paul. *The People of Concord*, Chester, Connecticut: Globe Pequot Press, 1990.

Brown, A. E. *History of the Town of Bedford*. Bedford, Massachusetts. Self-published. 1891.

Chamberlain, Samuel, *Lexington and Concord*. New York, New York: Hasting House, 1939.

Dublin, Thomas (ed.). *Immigrant Voices*. Urbana, Illinois: University of Illinois, 1993.

Dublin, Thomas (ed.). *Transforming Women's Work*. Ithaca, New York: Cornell University Press, 1994.

Egger-Bovet, Howard and Marle Smith-Baranzini, *US KIDS History: Book of the American Revolution*. Boston, Massachusetts; Little, Brown and Company, 1994.

Eisler, Benita (ed.). *The Lowell Offering*. New York, New York: Harper Colophon Books, 1977.

Fernald, Helen Clark. *Sketches of Old Lexington*. Hadley Press, Lexington, Massachusetts, c1930.

_____. *The Harrington House*. Lexington, Massachusetts, 1937.

Fisher, David Hackett, *Paul Revere's Ride*. New York, NY: Oxford University Press, 1994.

French, Allen, *Day of Concord and Lexington*. Boston, Massachusetts: Little, Brown, and Company, 1925.

French, Allen, *Historic Concord: A Handbook of Its Story and Its Memorials, with an Account of the Lexington Fight*. Concord, Massachusetts: Friends of the Concord Free Public Library, 1992. 2nd rev. ed./newly rev. by David B. Little.

Friends of the Bedford Free Public Library, *The Bedford Sampler Bicentennial Edition*, Bedford, Massachusetts, 1974.

Galvin, John. *The Minute Men: The First Fight-Myths and Realities of the American Revolution*. Washington: Brassey's, c1989.

Gara, Larry. *The Liberty Line*. Lexington, Kentucky: University of Kentucky Press, 1961.

Garrelick, Renee. *Clothier of the Assabet*. Concord, Massachusetts. Private, 1988.

_____. *Concord in the Days of Strawberries and Streetcars*. Concord: The Town of Concord. 1985.

Gross, Robert, *The Minutemen and Their World*. Greensboro, NC: Morgan Reynolds, Inc., 2001.

Henrick ,George and Willene. (ed.) *Fleeing For Freedom*. Chicago, Illinois: Ivan R. Dee, 2004.

Kehoe, Vincent. *The British Story of the Battle of Lexington and Concord*. Los Angeles, California: Hale & Co., 2000.

Kollen, Richard. *Lexington From Liberty's Birthplace to Progressive Suburb*. Charleston, Arcadia, 2004.

Lexington High School. *Investigating Lexington's History*. Lexington High School, 1998-2006.

Lexington Historical Society. *Proceedings, Vol 1-IV*. Lexington, Massachusetts, 1890-1910.

Little, David. *America's First Centennial Celebration*. Boston, MA: Houghton Mifflin Company, 1974.

Lothrop, Margaret. *The Wayside: Home of Authors*. New York, New York: American Book Company, 1940.

Mansur, Ina and Lawrence. *A Pictorial History of Bedford, Massachusetts, 1729 to Modern Times*. Barre, Vermont: Modern Printing Co., Inc. 1992.

Moran, William. *The Belles of New England*, New York, New York: Thomas Dunne Books, 2002.

Nelson, Liz. *Concord: Stories to Be Told*. Beverly, Massachusetts. Commonwealth Editions, 2002.

Petrulionis, Sandra H. *To Set This World Right*. Ithaca, New York: Cornell University Press, 2006.

_____. "Swelling That Great Tide of Humanity: The Concord, Massachusetts, Female Anti-Slavery Society," *The New England Quarterly*, Vol. 74, No. 3. (Sept., 2001), pp. 385-418.

Phinney, Elias. *History of the Battle of Lexington*. Boston, Massachusetts: Phelps and Farnham, 1825.

Porter, E.G. and H.M. Stephenson, *Souvenir of 1775: 1775-Lexington-1875*. Boston, Massachusetts: James R. Osgood & Co., 1875.

Pullen, D. Hinkle, A. and N. Buglar. *A Lexington Sampler for Children*. Lexington, Massachusetts: Battlegreen Publications, 1973.

Ris, Elisabeth. *Old Belfry Club*. Investigating American History. Lexington High School, 2001.

Robinson, Harriet. *Loom & Spindle*. Kailua, Hawaii, Press Pacifica, 1976.

Rooney, E. Ashley with Mary Martin. *Lexington to Concord: The Road to Independence in Postcards*. Atglen, Pennsylvania: Schiffer Publishing, 2007.

Ryan, D. Michael. *Concord and the Dawn of Revolution.* Charleston, South Carolina: The History Press, 2007.

Sellers-Garcie Oliver. *The Lexington Theater, Investigating American History.* Lexington High School, January 1998.

Shattuck, Lemuel. *History of the Town of Concord.* Boston, Massachusetts. Russell, Odiorne, and Company, 1835.

Sheton, Jane Deforest. *The Salt-Box House.* Charles Scribner's Sons, New York, NY, 1929.

Spevack, Edmund Charles. *Follen's Search for Nationality and Freedom.* Cambridge, Massachusetts: Harvard University Press, 1997.

Spidley, Jasneed. *Irish Immigration into Lexington.* Investigating American History, Lexington High School, January 1999.

Sullivan, Caitlin. *Irish in Lexington's History.* Investigating American History. Lexington High School, 2002.

Sullivan, E. O. *Time and the Tavern.* Lexington Historical Society, 1993.

Todd, Charles Burr. *In Olde Massachusetts.* New York, NY: The Grafton Press, 1971.

Tourtellot, Arthur Bernon, *Beginning of the War of the American Revolution.* New York, NY: W. W. Norton 1963, c1959.

Wallace, Teresa. Underground Railroad in Concord and at the Wayside, CRB1345244, 1997.

Webber, Joan W. *The Munroe Tavern.* Lexington, Massachusetts. Lexington Historical Society, 1976.

Wheeler, Ruth. *Concord: Climate for Freedom.* Concord, Massachusetts: The Concord Antiquarian Society, 1967.

Wilson, Leslie Perrin. *In History's Embrace.* Hollis, New Hampshire: Hollis Publishing, 2007.

Wilson, Sasha. *Entertainment in Lexington in 1920s.* Investigating American History, Lexington High School, 2006-2007.

Worthen, Edwin B. *A Calendar History of Lexington Massachusetts, 1620-1946.* Lexington, MA: Lexington Savings Bank, 1946.

Wright, Elizabeth. "Suburbanization and the Rural Domestic Ideal in Lexington." PhD. Thesis. Boston University. 1982.

Resources

Bedford Historical Society
Concord Library
Lexington Historical Society
Minute Man National Historical Park

Index